JAMES CARPENTER
ENVIRONMENTAL REFRACTIONS

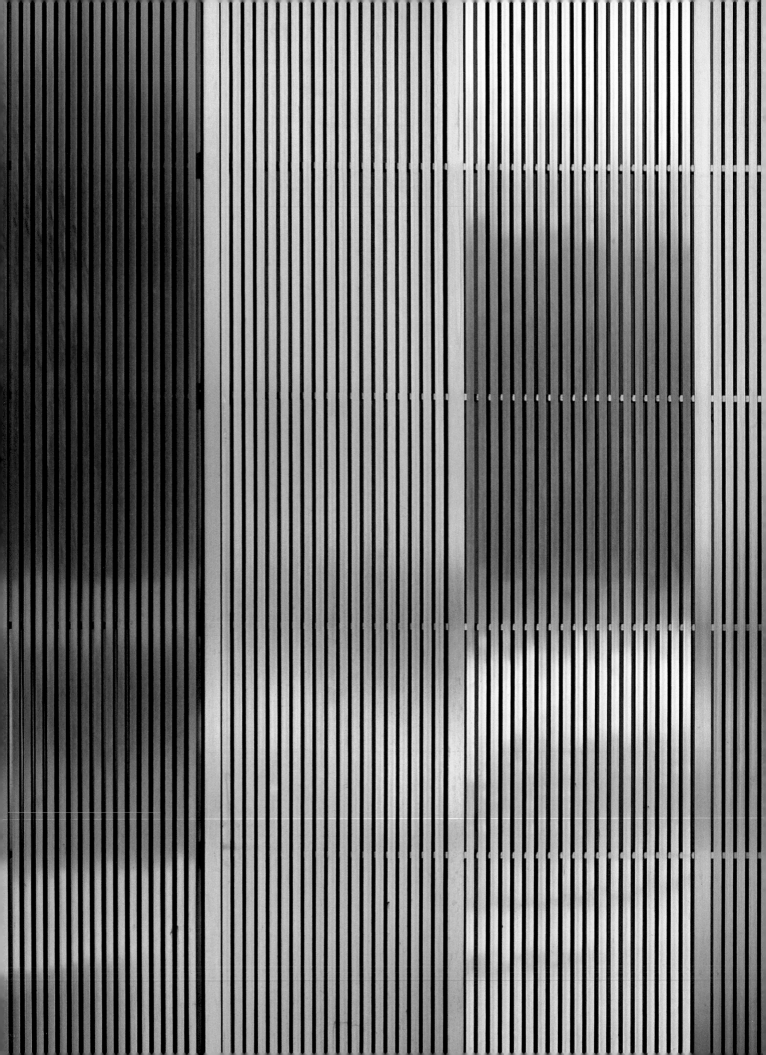

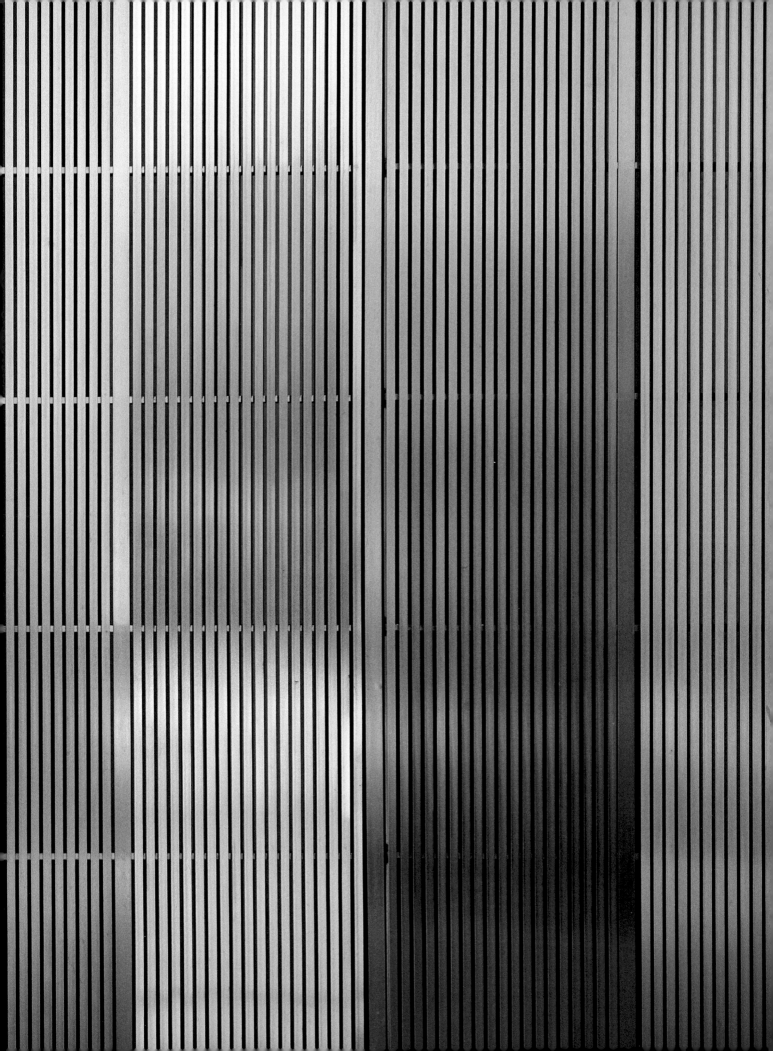

To Andrea and Linda, reaches of light and love

SANDRO MARPILLERO

James Carpenter

ENVIRONMENTAL REFRACTIONS

Preface by Jörg Schlaich
Essay by Kenneth Frampton

PRINCETON ARCHITECTURAL PRESS

New York

First published in North and South America in 2006 by
Princeton Architectural Press
37 East Seventh Street
New York, New York 10003

For a free catalog of books, call 1.800.722.6657.
Visit our Web site at www.papress.com.

First published outside North and South America in 2006 by
Birkhäuser – Publishers for Architecture
P.O. Box 133, CH-4010
Basel, Switzerland
www.birkhauser.ch

© 2006 Birkhäuser – Publishers for Architecture
Part of Springer Science+Business Media
Printed and bound in Germany
09 08 07 06 4 3 2 1 First edition

For Birkhäuser – Publishers for Architecture

Graphic design: nalbach typografik, Stuttgart
Volker Kühn, Silke Nalbach

Project management: Ben Colebrook, JCDA
Assistant to author: Laura Crescimano

Lithography: Repromayer, Reutlingen
Printing: Leibfarth & Schwarz, Dettingen / Erms
Silkscreen cover: Gerscher Druck, Aglasterhausen

Library of Congress Cataloging-in-Publication Data
Marpillero, S. (Sandro)
James Carpenter: environmental refractions | Sandro Marpillero
preface by Jörg Schlaich | essay by Kenneth Frampton.
p. cm.
Includes bibliographical references.
ISBN-13: 978-1-56898-608-1 (alk. paper)
ISBN-10: 1-56898-608-4 (alk. paper)
1. Carpenter, James, 1949– –Criticism and interpretation.
2. Glass construction. 3. Glass sculpture. 4. Light in architecture.
I. Title: Environmental refractions. II. Carpenter, James, 1949–
III. Frampton, Kenneth. IV. Title.
NA737.C267.M37 2006
720.92–dc22
2006001272

CONTENTS

WORKING WITH JAMES CARPENTER

by Jörg Schlaich

James Carpenter has freed me from a prejudice. As an engineer designing civil engineering projects (in my case mainly bridges and lightweight shells with wide spans), I formerly forbade myself the use of design resources for their own sake. In keeping with this conviction, not even the individual details of a design were to be shaped by a pure desire for aesthetic expression, but were instead always clearly subordinated to or derived from function: the conceptual formulation program, the location, the flow of forces, the manufacturing technology. Everything else was regarded as decoration, as "wallpaper," and hence as inadmissible, dishonest, insincere.

For me, art and architecture, and likewise art and civil engineering, were never entirely separate, but my inspiring collaborations with James Carpenter have allowed the boundaries between the two to become more fluid, thereby opening up new design possibilities for me. Of course, it remains true for me that not only architecture, but also civil engineering projects such as bridges, should primarily serve their users. People should feel comfortable with them, and should enjoy identifying with their designs both as a whole and in detail; they should also be economically feasible. The current trend to design trendy sculptures solely in order to showcase the architect, and with no regard for social context, has nothing to do with genuine architecture and architectural culture, not to mention many over-designed "landmark bridges," which will doubtless have very short lifespans.

The external form of a functional structure serves the noble purpose of addressing the beholder in a way that goes beyond function, of narrating its own history, of delighting or conveying some artistic expression. Why then, we ask ourselves with good reason, should we not call for more generous budgets for them when purely "autonomous" art is held in such high esteem? In fact, such demands have been long recognized when it comes to museums, banks, and large office buildings, and they play an increasing role in the selection of a design. But the more obviously the functional purpose of a building steps into the foreground, the smaller the role of aesthetic aspects. Such considerations, hence, rarely come into play with bridges, for example (aside from a few celebrated exceptions), against which many sins have been committed under the pretense of the imperatives of permanence and economic efficiency. But anything created by human beings may be a work of art, even a bridge.

A striking instance of the interplay between construction and art, and one that emerged from a collaboration with James Carpenter, is the roof and façade of the Lichthof (atrium) of the German Foreign Ministry in Berlin. For this building, we designed a filigree cable-net façade whose transparency and lightness strives to dissolve the boundary separating the atrium from the outside.

In Berlin, James Carpenter revealed to us the artistic potential of this façade, a dimension he was able to disclose without—and this is the decisive aspect—sacrificing any structural aspects. He designed a flowing transition from a pure construction via civil engineering to art, so that façade and glass roof not only serve a rational purpose, but bear an expression as well. The construction becomes a component of a powerful work of art, and the additional expense (coated glass, a few strips of reflective metal, dichroic glass, together with stainless steel struts between the virtual vertical and horizontal façade cables) is relatively minor, yet it converts light into an active design element by means of an interplay of multifaceted chromatic reflections.

Somewhat later, we worked together with the architects of SOM and James Carpenter in planning a highly transparent cable-net façade for the Time Warner building on Columbus Circle in New York City, and behind this, a façade that serves as acoustic insulation for the Jazz@Lincoln Center performance space. Here Carpenter allowed the pure construction and unobstructed views onto 58th Street to speak, absent any additional elements: engineering as art. This reticence, where pure construction is deemed sufficient, this preparedness and capacity to listen, and to allow oneself to be stimulated by a profound understanding of construction that is impelled by curiosity before making one's own proposals: all of this is characteristic of James Carpenter's definition of fruitful collaboration.

Many contemporary architects imagine themselves capable of devising designs precisely in areas where they lack the requisite competence, only to wind up copying the preexistent, while simultaneously underestimating the importance of construction and diminishing the role of the engineer to mere structural calculations. In contrast, James Carpenter regards the knowledge and ideas of his design partners as grist for his own mill, fusing them with his own fantasy and artistic gifts—in the knowledge that pure, effective, skillful, and intelligent construction provides fertile ground for art.

«What else can I know and do… except measure the relationship between the secret which is entombed in the stone and the one which lies in the worker that transforms it into a building?»

MICHEL SERRES | *What Thales Saw at the Base of the Pyramids*

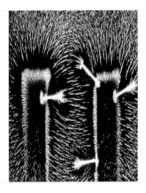

Iron filings under the influence of a magnetic field.

The appearance of James Carpenter's work is serene. It gives the impression, however, that something new will happen amidst its supposed serenity, and that other forces – apart from those already apparent – are about to enter its field. The work produces an *inhabited depth*, by shifting emphasis away from the visual registers of perception, towards multiple engagements of a subject, her/his spatial constructs, and their resulting environment. Carpenter addresses the object of perception not only by positioning it within cultural and economic contexts, but also by inscribing it into biological and ecological systems. His work challenges a conventional description of its forms, which also implicates the techniques through which architecture organizes the disciplinary controls of that which exceeds its limits.

The interaction between the visual and bodily dimensions of Carpenter's work promotes an approach to architecture that I will call "environmental." The production of a vast array of interferences destabilizes the aesthetic autonomy of its objects of perception – an autonomy that has persisted as one of the enduring myths of architecture. His concerns also highlight the idea that addressing sustainable resources should not remain narrowly focused on conventional notions of building technology, nor limit that focus to the performance of some materials. Buildings are implicated in actively constructing cities and landscapes, and should be made accountable for the way in which they invest urban contexts beyond historical nostalgia, and its associated longing for pastoral landscapes. The notion of environment that emerges from these premises points towards the establishment of new ecological paradigms focused on dynamic transformations, rather than the preservation of an idealized nature.

This book presents a part of Carpenter's vast and heterogeneous production, within this framework of an environmental approach, by identifying three groups of works that pose significant questions to architectural as well as art practices.

The first challenge in inscribing Carpenter's work within this environmental approach results from the perverse resistance offered by photography to the power of the work's spatial and material dimensions. Photographs can only offer a limited translation of the properties through which the work engages and affects its surroundings. They tend to freeze the palpable tension between the work's apparent geometrical necessity and its articulation of multiple experiential registers. They also flatten the appreciation of models and built pieces to a phenomenological reading of their materiality.

In each of the book's three sections, an introduction addresses one or several selected projects, which have been chosen as paradigmatic of the challenges raised by specific aspects of Carpenter's work. Each introduction includes a short discussion of the analytic diagrams which are part of that section's interpretive framework. These diagrams serve to shift attention to the work's operational aspects rather than focusing on its physical properties, as photographs and line drawings would tend to encourage.

SECTION I: REFRACTIONS

Section I focuses on the way in which Carpenter's work constructs physical and conceptual frameworks through which the phenomenon of refraction operates within the perceptual field of subject/object relationships. *Periscope Window* (1994–1998) and *Dichroic Light Field* (1995–1996) are the two projects chosen to bracket this phenomenon, which exceeds in each case its respective emphasis on an experience of transparency and reflectivity. These two works of Carpenter's represent artistic essays on the way in which glass can heighten dynamic shifts in the temporally conditioned relationship between subject and object.

Refraction, in literal terms, occurs when a ray of light is deflected from its previous trajectory as it passes from one medium into another of different density. Conceptually, refraction is a spatial construct that activates vision as a process mediated by materiality. It affects the constitution of subjectivity through an oscillation between physical and imaginary registers. With refraction, the properties of glass transform the role of the observer into that of an active interpreter. Carpenter's investment in the materiality of glass effects this transformation.

Both *Periscope Window* and *Dichroic Light Field* explore the tension introduced within their material frames by internal and external agencies. This exploration acknowledges that the forces at play within the field of perception belong to different orders of reality, transforming it into a battlefield between cultural conventions and unconscious impulses.

SECTION II: CONSTRUCTIONS

Section II posits that Carpenter's work probes the rhetoric of transparency within architecture's modernist tradition to the point of undermining the association between the relative stability of a building and its monumental permanence. Carpenter's contribution to *7 World Trade Center* in Lower Manhattan introduces conceptual disjunctions in the perception of the building's envelope and spatial transitions, which places into crisis the idea of pure transparency – from both a visual and material point of view—by introducing tensions and interferences between temporal and spatial variables.

This project is a window into a context of codified relationships as they relate to the construction of a high-rise building, revealing how Carpenter has operated through and beyond the typical configuration of design processes and their conventional protocols of collaboration. The fast-track schedule of design, development, and implementation of *7 WTC* has been accompanied by subtle variations along lines of conduct as well as dynamic crossovers between architectural, engineering, and artistic fields of practice.

The role of Carpenter's work in glass and steel within this process of multiple collaborations suggests the possibility of moving away from the nineteenth and early twentieth century notion of tectonics as a utilitarian function of technology towards its redefinition through the contemporary questions raised by the preeminence of images and messages. It also posits challenges to the way in which the discipline of architecture has cultivated design authorship and illusions of control on building processes, that belong to outmoded artistic and social formations.

SECTION III: APPARATUSES

Following the critique of the rhetoric of transparency in architecture and its related notion of object, Section III interrogates how Carpenter's work might operate as an apparatus within a complex field of environmental fluxes.

The apparently heterogeneous work chosen to introduce this section focuses on the production of effects that migrate from visual and imaginary registers towards a physical awareness of bodily sensations in space. Carpenter's early installations of short films, *Cause, Confines, Koi, Homing,* and *Migration* (1975–1980) introduce a cinematic paradigm that is detectable in his more recent projects. The early films, as projected in art galleries, manipulated the ecological content of the work in such a way as to viscerally implicate a visitor in the space of the gallery itself. It is through the environmental register inherent in these installations that Carpenter entered the field of architecture, eventually collaborating in the design of the *Tulane University Student Center* (1999–2006). For the Tulane University project Carpenter developed aspects of building systems as hybrid constructs, that could make an observer reconsider her/his spatial conceptions, by focusing on environmental information and forces observed countless times without noticing. As a working assemblage of elements, these constructs can operate as apparatuses, by positioning them within

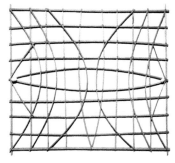

a relational framework that opens architecture to changes over time. The regions of reality engaged by these apparatuses are conceptually incommensurable to one another, while, at the same time, affecting the quality of a subject's awareness of her/his surroundings.

NAVIGATION

The book's organization is not a linear sequence of projects ordered in accordance with chronological, typological, or thematic classification of built and unbuilt structures. Rather than a geometry, the book attempts a geography of the work's possible arrays: a mapping that articulates aspects of possible interpretation, rather than precisely described formal or functional attributes. Navigation rather than genealogical classification is the analog for the book's approach to Carpenter's work, and as such it suggests a counterpoint to the inevitable linearity of editorial formats. While the individual texts describe the projects' focus on their specific agendas, which are not homogeneous within any of the three sections, the diagrams that accompany the projects chosen as paradigms suggest cross references among them.

Stick charts produced by ancient mariners from the Marshall Islands in the Pacific South West offer an image for this framework of navigation. These nautical aids indicate the reflection and cross interaction of ocean swells between atolls and other island formations: the sticks are patterns of swells between particular atolls—themselves indicated by small shells. A navigator would work out from a given swell pattern his probable position among these low and strung-out islands, not visible above the sea surface for many miles. In the book, paradigmatic projects play this role of navigational reference; the projects that follow them in each section have been collected by keeping in mind this conceptual framework, in light of the possibility that other affinities may pull a reader toward alternative overlapping routes.

The project for a *Luminous Glass Bridge* (1987) exemplifies the potential for such affinities and overlaps. The bridge's technical aspects—cantilevered and offset abutments, cable structure and post-tensioned deck—reflect Carpenter's early interest in engineering and relate it to issues addressed in Section II. At the same time, engineering operates in this project as an apparatus in the environmental sense: the cable above the platform is not only used to enhance the glass deck's stability and functionality, but also to secure at the top and bottom three pivoting vertical plates of glass. The panels enable a pedestrian's passage while a special coating on their surfaces reflects fleeting images of the landscape that extends beyond each side of the canyon. The engagement of phenomena and flows operating at a scale larger than the one implied by a simple physical crossing could therefore suggest positioning this project in Section III.

The *Luminous Glass Bridge* is placed instead in Section I, prioritizing its more obvious intensification of a pedestrian's perceptual awareness of crossing the river. Because of its reflection and projection of the shimmering of the water below, the bridge joins the other projects exploring refraction, and ends Section I as an announcement of the engineering and environmental focus of the two following sections. Through this provisional placement, the *Glass Bridge* is cast as a clue of Carpenter's own creative route that, over the past 25 years, has moved away from the self-referential domain of artistic glass objects towards a broader agenda and a closer integration with the process of conception and development of architectural design.

I REFRACTIONS

«Generally speaking, the relation between the gaze and what one wishes to see involves a lure. The subject is presented as other than he is, and what one shows him is not what he wishes to see.»

JACQUES LACAN | The Four Fundamental Concepts of Psychoanalysis

The first section of this book frames Carpenter's work as a process of transformation of the phenomena of transparency and reflectivity. In order to qualify the notion of refraction that emerges from this process, I will begin with a piece from one of his rare interviews:

Northern Labrador...that there are very small communities of Eskimos, and Indians, of maybe...of forty or one hundred people, two hundred miles away from each other...was helping a family to keep up their fishing, somehow taking the soul's place...they were on the water at night in a small boat. In Labrador they...squid...squid that come in at night. Millions of squid, underneath the boat...turned into this completely luminescent surface that produced a physical vortex. Things like that vibrate and are quite amazing...the...the memory of something like that, in a very abstract way, has given me a...to think about making things that could heighten people's awareness of phenomena...it is occurring out there all the time.

In this account, Carpenter's nearness to the squid's nocturnal vision is not only physical, but also influenced by his participation in the productive activities of a societal group with which he has formed a familial kinship. His position within this cultural field displaces his geometric control over the object of perception, configuring more complex interactions with the world's images and realities. The shimmering of these living entities becomes a source of light, manifesting the relevance of the environmental dynamics from which they arise, as a lure towards a deeper involvement with the act of vision. As a viewer seduced to venture into the depth of the elusive confines of their image, Carpenter establishes a condition of reciprocity between the field, which is perspectively centered on himself at its origin, and the complex dynamics of transparency and reflectivity which allow the object of perception to "look back" at him.
There is a qualitative difference between the way an observer can idealize an object, and the development of a productive knowledge with respect to an object's ideality on the part of a maker. The idealization of an object by a viewer can embed its perception in a network of resonant memories. This quantity of memory eventually gives way to an imaginary relation, by substituting one apparent sense for another.
As a maker, Carpenter recasts the role of the observer through multiple investigations that establish a relationship between vision and the natural environment, qualified by observing light as part

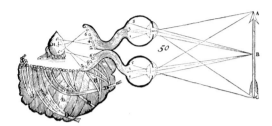

of a thick vibrating field. The choice of glass as privileged medium for his work has allowed him, since the period of his artistic education at the Rhode Island School of Design, to explore the interaction between this material's supposed transparency and the conceptual thickness it can induce in the perception of various phenomena. In doing so, he has transformed the mysterious luminescence of the school of squid seen in Labrador into temporally shifting figures of light.

In this transformation of light from its literal rendition (as a light emitting diode) into an abstraction (as a luminous solar body) that appears between, before, and behind him, as that which is passing through the material, and as that component of light activated by the material ... We see individually, brings to view the paradoxical transparence and, simultaneously, making public in the inner workings in practice of refraction and reflection.

I have chosen two of Carpenter's projects in order to introduce the notion of refraction as a key to this complex field of vision. The first project, *Periscope Window* (1994–1998), takes the place of a window within a private residence; the second, *Dichroic Light Field* (1995–1996), layers a field of mirroring surfaces on an urban wall. Both works explore how the use of glass can modify the relationship between subject and object through effects which are produced within and through the glass's own materiality. The operations through which glass produces refraction in these two projects transform the material into a perceptual device that actively participates in the process of image formation. Images are affected by the technical properties of the device, including the type of glass, the substructure, and the method of construction, as well as its relation with time of day or night, season, weather, and its modes of spatial engagement with the human body.

These two works, while manifesting their affinity with the transparency of glass and the reflectivity of mirrors, also address two established architectural tropes—window and wall—reconsidering their conventional roles in delineating boundaries between inside and outside. Carpenter's installations problematize the way in which architecture is organized as a linguistic system of identifiable and discrete elements. Both *Periscope Window* and *Dichroic Light Field* are interventions integrated into the real space of architecture through partial reconstructions that modify the transparency, opacity, and reflectivity of the buildings to which they are applied. They produce an oscillation within the perceptual field, which becomes a source of uncertainty, operating—so to speak—from underneath its threshold of visibility.

Rather than a direct relationship with objects, these complex dynamics of transfomation introduce a perceptual delay in the identification of a discrete object, shifting this process towards a subject's imaginary dimensions. As opposed to the fixity of an ideal eye, these perceptual oscillations promote spatial memories in which a subject's layered experiences allow time to make irruption into the supposed immediacy of vision. Carpenter's work asserts that spatial experiences need to be re-inscribed in the temporal web of multiple projections of a body in its process of constitution. The work also makes manifest that these projections are affected by the opaque regions of unconscious interferences.

PERISCOPE WINDOW

Looked at in isolation, the device of *Periscope Window* displays a level of material and constructive elegance that alone would generate sufficient focus of attention as an object in a museum. However, this engineered construction of glass, crystal lenses, and mirrors has been designed to interact with the mutable environment of a precise place and time. These interactions produce multiple effects that are layered on the device's visible surface of acid-etched glass, and, at the same time, thwart the drive towards its reduction to the status of artistic commodity in a private home.

In architectural terms, *Periscope Window* confronts the conventional idea that a window presents a framed view from a building interior to its exterior, directly connected with the outside through the stability of the window's frame and of the horizon line in relation to the floor. In classical terms, a window's vertical axis stabilizes a subject's position through perspectival vision. In its modernist reformulation, a window's horizontal extension promotes instead a cinematic mode of perception of the exterior. Carpenter subverts the window's direct connection to the outside, presupposed by both classical and modernist paradigms. Despite being faced by the neighbor's adjacent fence, the *Periscope Window's* thickness enables it to absorb the view of a tree beyond the fence, endowing the tree with the power of casting shadows, simulating a solar eclipse, and projecting a picture on the window's inner plane. The changing quality of these indirect images, compounded by other perceptual variables, intensifies the relationship between the viewer, the device, and environmental events such as cloud variations and solar movement.

Operating at multiple scales to produce co-present images through different optical processes, *Periscope Window* shifts emphasis away from the accepted notions of a window as an architectural frame separating the inside from the outside. The glass thus acquires a life of its own as the source of a dynamic accumulation of perceptions that bring together conceptually incommensurable images. A geometry of intensive forces connects these images in a network of changing and developing relations. Light is treated as a potent vector of intensity: the visible comes into existence only through light's thickening and confrontation with shadows–a shifting and unstable chiaroscuro. Light becomes visible by reaching a sensation of brilliance that is at the same time a source of pleasure and pain for the eye. Scintillating phenomena of flickers and halos foreground the forces animating the natural world outside the building.

DICHROIC LIGHT FIELD

Whereas *Periscope Window* captures and relays convergent aspects of phenomena through mirrors and lenses, *Dichroic Light Field* operates as a geometric device that registers environmental energies in a way that produces a different order of time-related phenomena.

The work consists of planes of specially treated glass that appear to trap light, giving an illusion of depth. The observer and the perceived objects are in this case on "the same side" relative to the protruding components of the device–216 dichroic laminated glass fins. Yet the mutual interaction between elements and the wall that is their supporting plane produces a large and subtle range of effects, in which each element assumes a crucial role. Meanwhile, the effects of solar movement and weather conditions are multiplied by the distance, direction, and speed of the movements of an observer, who shares the urban context of the piece.

In *Dichroic Light Field*, duration is an effect of the activation of selective reflections of the glistening context and the highlighting of that process of activation. Nearby buildings become a source of light by reflecting towards Carpenter's device the afternoon sun that shines on their façades. The resulting effects depend on multiple combinations among perceptual variables. For example, two individuals observing the work at the same time from the north and the south would see two radically different images.

The work's geometric configuration interacts with multiple factors (lighting, space, angles of sun and vision, distance, objects, and interrelated movements) which affect, through their own variations, the transformations of one image into another within a modular field. The aesthetic effect is an image of movement of a changing whole that is produced through geometric figures co-present to one another. Light is conceived as a function of movement, correlating an infinite display of successive moments through the viewer's perceptual mobility in front of a regularized field of light figures.

DIAGRAMS

Three types of diagrams guide the interpretation of *Periscope Window* and *Dichroic Light Field.* Since a key component in both works is time—as measured and qualified by the movement of the sun—one set of diagrams depicts the sun's hourly and seasonal positions in relation to the orientation of both devices.

A second set of diagrams describes how phenomena engaged by each device in terms of action and context are perceived. In the case of *Periscope Window*, images express the dynamic quality of time through an intensification of effects of light and shadow. In the case of *Dichroic Light Field*, the quality of time is instead expressed through images extracted in an almost mathematical way from the movement of sunlight. Both sets of diagrams could seem to share an affinity with the abstraction of orthographic projections. Yet the way in which these conventions of representation are used here undermines their analytical and pictorial temptations, since these two devices precisely investigate the variability, relativity, and interaction that take place in the act of perception. In other words, the intent of the diagrams is to show the way in which these two works operate on vision itself.

In the case of *Periscope Window,* the frontal relation between a viewer in the private residence's stairwell and the tree outside, in the neighbor's property, is rendered through axonometric drawings. These static and analytical representations of both the architectural support and its view of nature also freeze the outline of subject and object, highlighting the fact that the sun is the primary variable of the perceptual situation.

These axonometric drawings are complemented by a third set of related diagrams. Detailed sections through the window follow the different trajectories of light—modified by the components that construct the window as a device. These sections are paired with the undoing of a single image into three different parts that correspond to the principal effects of shadow, eclipse, and projection produced by the device.

The second set of diagrams illustrating the *Dichroic Light Field* addresses photography's reduction of the work's spatial and temporal depth to a sequence of beautiful images. The purpose of these "lateral perspectives" is to investigate the optical illusionism of both constructed perspectival drawings and photographic images.

They establish a conceptual difference between the disembodied subject of idealized representations and the process through which the work's surface can absorb a subject within its depth confirming its imaginary presence. Once perspective is understood as a construct, it can redefine space as an opportunity for a complex dialogue that projects a subject along the vectors of her/

his possible desires. These vectors probe the elusive depth of the picture's planar coordinates through an uneven field of *here* and *there*. As a device, the *Dichroic Light Field* implicates the eye of a distracted passer-by, transforming the act of viewing it into the specific temporality of a subject's situation.

Brunelleschi conducted an analogous experiment in Florence, when he invited passers-by to slip behind a device that produced an unprecedented view of urban spaces. Viewers were asked to hold a mirror in front of a perspectival drawing, so that they could observe this image within the context of the physical reality of the square in which they were. The final picture required an observer to move her/his body, in order to adjust the relative size of the images corresponding to each element. The resulting view through Brunelleschi's device was in fact an assemblage of surfaces that put into relief simultaneously the drawing of the Baptistery and the square in which it was, including the cathedral, so as to prevent the Baptistery's reduction to an abstracted urban object. Within this view, cast shadows and the moving clouds in the sky were potent indexes of the picture's embodied temporality.

---

[1] See Pia Sarpaneva, "Interview with James Carpenter," *Presence Symposium*, Blacksburg: College of Architecture and Urban Studies of Virginia Tech, 1998, p.6.

[2] Pia Sarpaneva, op. cit, p.8.

PERISCOPE WINDOW

Minneapolis | Minnesota | 1995–1997

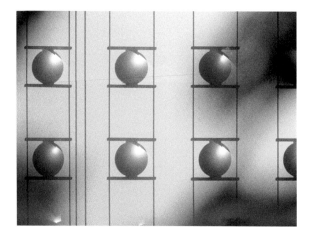 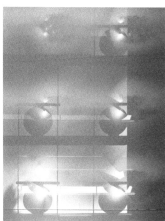

∧ As the morning progresses direct light reaches more and more of the acid-etched glass, erasing any projected imagery other than the sun from the lenses becoming a bright screen for the shadows cast from the tree, passing clouds, the installation's structure and its lenses.

↘ Diagram showing the difference between the phenomenon of transparency and the effect of refraction produced by the Periscope Window.

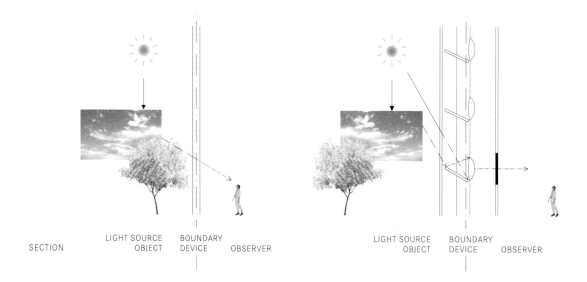

SECTION LIGHT SOURCE OBJECT BOUNDARY DEVICE OBSERVER   LIGHT SOURCE OBJECT BOUNDARY DEVICE OBSERVER

The Periscope Window reveals the outside world in the form of shadows cast onto it, while the lenses simultaneously project an image whose upended horizon suggests a world apart. Located in the stairway of a private residence and facing a view obstructed by a fence, only feet away, and the neighboring building beyond, the Periscope Window creates a richly textured "view," layering variously scaled representations of the exterior phenomenon.

Based on earlier lens projects, Carpenter's team designed this structure to act like a periscope device. The effect was achieved by adjusting the operable parts—two layers of glass 12 inch (304mm) apart, 14 suspended horizontal

mirrors angled, and 80 glass lenses—to the specific site conditions. The interior glass, seen from inside the house, is a projection screen consisting of specially treated layers of acid-etched, laminated glass panels. To avoid having to look at the nearby fence, mirrors are angled on the exterior side of the lenses; views of the sky and trees are interpreted by the lenses and then projected onto the window's plane. Each optical lens focuses an image of the sky and trees onto the inside of the laminated acid-etched glass, creating a grid of slightly different views of the same scene. The Window operates similarly at night, displaying images of the moon and night sky, including projections of tree branch shadows.

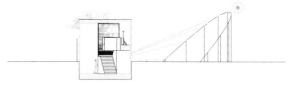

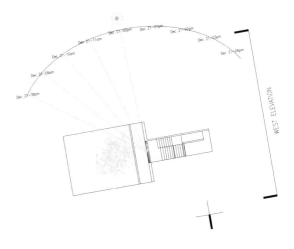

WINTER – DEC 21

WINTER – DEC 21

WEST ELEVATION

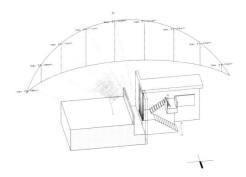

WINTER – DEC 21

∧ View of Periscope Window and neighboring fence.

> These diagrams of the Periscope Window's relationship to the site and to the passage of the sun through the sky on the summer and winter solstices describe the range and frequency of light phenomena captured by the window.

The architect, Vincent James, responded to the clients' desire for a calm and secluded residence in a densely populated neighborhood by significantly re-grading the site, thereby establishing a ground plane for the house that would selectively frame views, especially of an adjacent lake. One window on a staircase leading up to the second floor promised views of light filtering through the trees but was blocked by the neighboring building and nearby fence. In confronting this limitation, JCDA saw an opportunity to further alter the experience of "viewing."

SUMMER

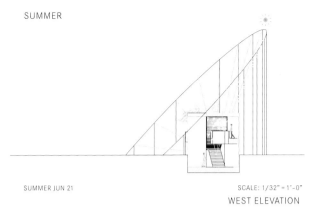

SUMMER JUN 21

SCALE: 1/32" = 1'-0"

WEST ELEVATION

∧ View from the south elevation of the house. The Periscope Window is located on the east side of the house.

∨ Behind the exterior insulated glass are the tension rods, horizontal mirrors, and cast glass lenses.

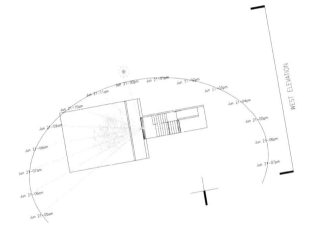

SUMMER JUN 21

SCALE: 1/32" = 1'-0"

PLAN

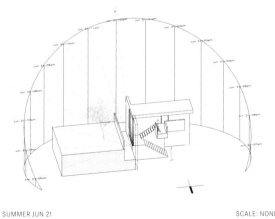

SUMMER JUN 21

SCALE: NONE

NORTH VIEW

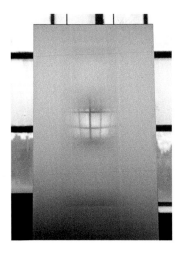

∧ The earliest mock-up established the lens's focal length and the necessary balance of translucency and transparency for the laminated acid-etched glass.

⌐ The supporting structure for the lenses was developed from the first mock-up. A layer of float glass custom laminated to a layer of acid-etched glass transforms the window into a screen, capturing reflections and projections.

> A blue panel, standing in for the sky, and three white squares, representing clouds, were mounted above and behind this working mock-up to examine how the angle of the mirrors and their distance from the lenses could transform a conventional view through the window into views of the nearby tree and the sky.

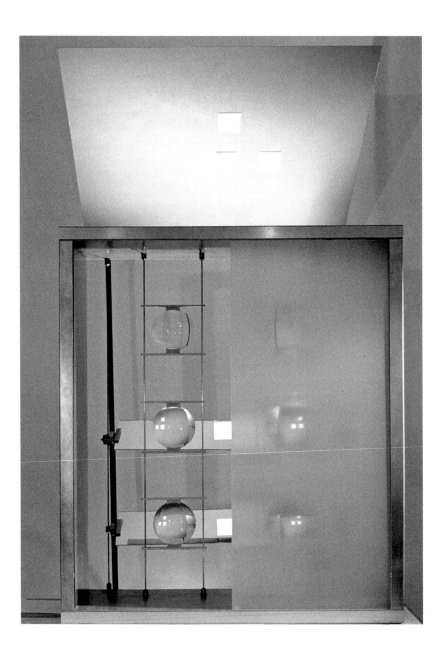

∨ This view during installation shows the edge of the property, marked by a large fence, and the clear view of the neighboring buildings. A stainless steel frame provides the structure for both the tensioned stainless steel rods that support the 80 lenses and 14 angled mirrors.

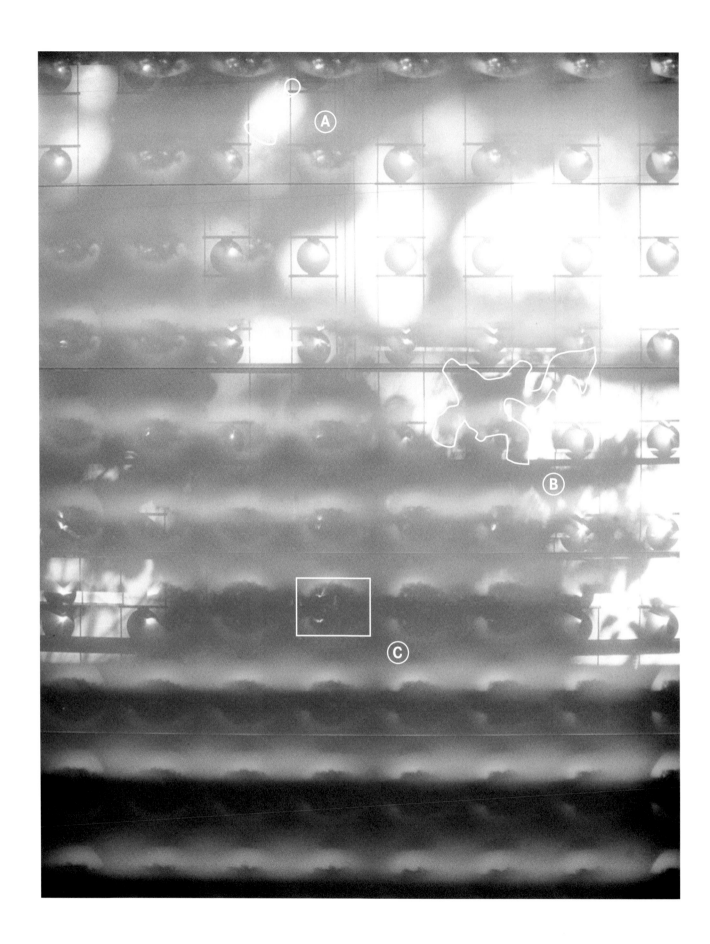

^ On a sunny summer morning the window captures the greatest number of phenomena, thereby generating the most layered image, including the revelation of some parts of the sculpture's structure and lenses. The diagrams isolate those phenomena and explain how and under what conditions they appear on various parts of the acid-etched glass.

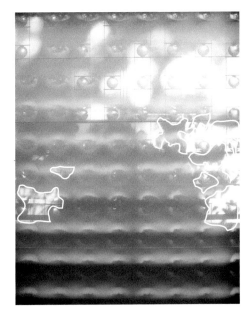

A PINHOLE PROJECTION
Overlapping or punctured leaves create tiny pinholes which act like lenses, focusing the direct image of the sun on the diffused glass surface. Without the Periscope Window this phenomenon is normally only observed during an eclipse.

B DIRECT SHADOW
Direct shadows are cast onto the acid-etched glass from obstructions such as clouds or, as in this case, the leaves and branches of the trees above and beyond the fence.

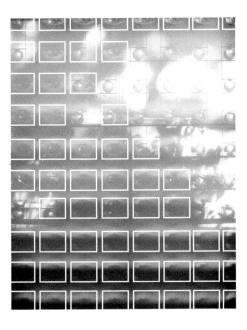

C LENS PROJECTION
The lenses project the mirrors' reflected images of sky and trees onto the acid-etched glass screen, rendering video monitor-like images of the tree-tops and sky beyond.

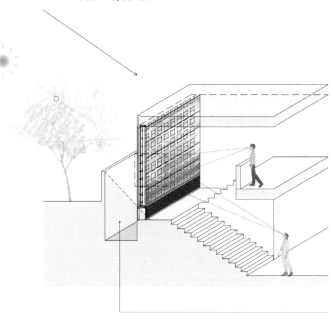

A PINHOLE PROJECTION

The distance between the pinhole and the screen determines the size of that projection. The pinhole projections of the sun's image move in the opposite direction of the sun and, because of the leaves' movements, flicker on and off. The interruptions cast by the structure, mirrors, and lenses add further texture and movement.

B DIRECT SHADOW

The light traveling from the sun is filtered by the tree: some light is completely blocked and some gets through creating a shadow whose outline of branches and leaves is cast onto the acid-etched screen. The lens and mirror projection is less visible, casting some of the sky image onto the shadow and reducing the shadow's contrast. The movement of the leaves adds an active sense of the tree's presence.

C LENS PROJECTION

The lenses project the mirrors' reflected images of sky and tree onto the acid-etched screen. The filtered light coming through the tree shades parts of the acid-etched glass, enabling it to capture the imagery projected by the lenses. The reversed images and representations of movement of the mirrors are inverted and reversed by the lenses, creating a correctly oriented but reversed moving image on the projection screen.

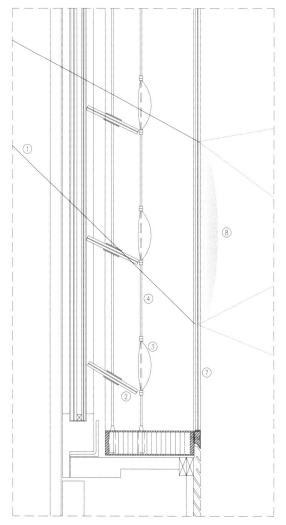

OPTICAL DEVICE – SINGLE LENS REFLEX

1 LIGHT & IMAGE SOURCE	5 FOCAL LENGTH
2 MIRROR (ANGLE VIEW TO LENS)	6 CAPACITY/REFRECTION OF LENS
3 CAST GLASS LENS (CAPTURED VIEW)	7 DIFFUSED GLASS (TREATED LAMINATED)
4 SUPPORTING TENSION ROD	8 PROJECTED IMAGE ON DIFFUSED GLASS

B DIRECT SHADOW

C LENS PROJECTION

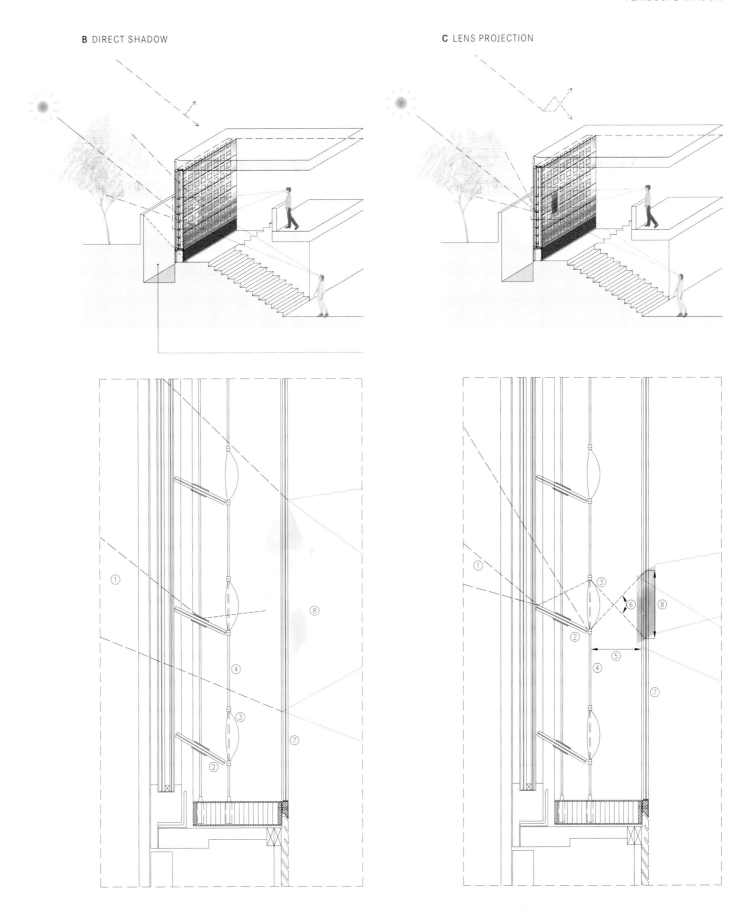

DICHROIC LIGHT FIELD

New York | New York | 1994–1995

Dichroic Light Field is an installation of glass fins on the east side of the Millenium Tower at 160 Columbus Avenue, New York, built in 1994–1995. The intent of the Dichroic Light Field was to break down the monolithic and opaque character of a block long brick façade by establishing an illusion of depth. The design sought to dissolve the wall itself while creating a cinematic frame on which the phenomena of projected imagery and light could be displayed.

Carpenter's team chose materials that would trace the sun's movement across the city and the pedestrians' shifting points of view as they walk past. The vertical density of the neighborhood often casts the street in shadow, emphasizing the theatrical nature of the city streetscape. By transforming the available light, the installation's reflective surfaces call attention to the phenomena of light while also reflecting that light to illuminate the street as much as possible.

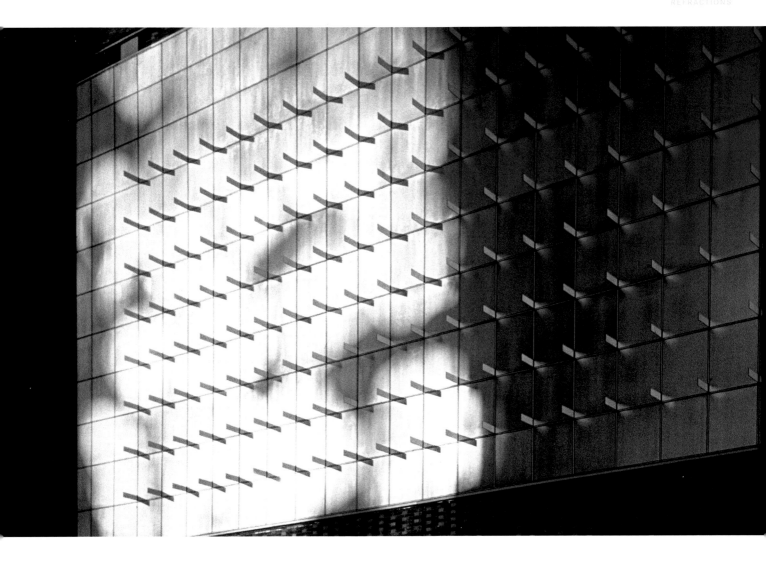

^ Secondary bounced light from an adjacent building activates the glass plane.

> Diagram showing the difference between the phenomenon of reflection and the effect of diffraction produced by the Dichroic Light Field.

⌐ Detail of the fins photographed at the same time from the north and from the south in bright yet overcast conditions.

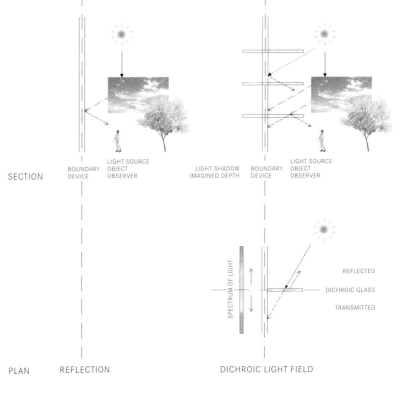

SECTION

BOUNDARY
DEVICE

LIGHT SOURCE
OBJECT
OBSERVER

LIGHT SHADOW
IMAGINED DEPTH

BOUNDARY
DEVICE

LIGHT SOURCE
OBJECT
OBSERVER

SPECTRUM OF LIGHT

REFLECTED

DICHROIC GLASS

TRANSMITTED

PLAN

REFLECTION

DICHROIC LIGHT FIELD

∧ ⊿ These two identical views from the south, seen early in the morning and close to noon, demonstrate how the installation dissolves the expanse of brick, reflects light and color, and acts as a screen framing light in its urban context.

⤓ > These diagrams illustrate the range of direct light and shadow that reaches the Dichroic Light Field at the winter and summer solstice.

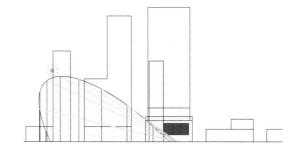

WINTER – DEC 21

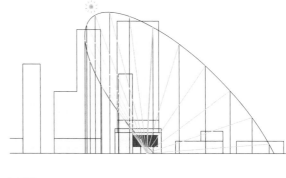

SUMMER JUN 21

SOUTH-EAST ELEVATION

As in the Periscope Window, the Dichroic Light Field responds to the specific nature of the setting. Gary Edward Handel & Associates' design of Millennium Tower created a monumental brick façade on the east side of the building to be occupied by an artwork. James Carpenter Design Associates presented the winning entry to the competition organized by the developer.

JCDA analyzed the installation's specific location and identified the area's urban topography to create a design that would register the cyclical passage of time and also map the local urban fabric.

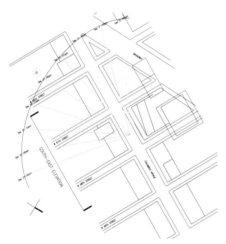

WINTER – DEC 21

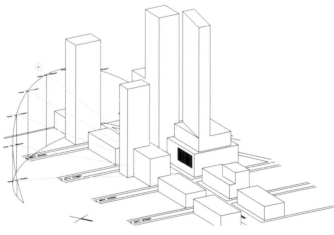

WINTER – DEC 21

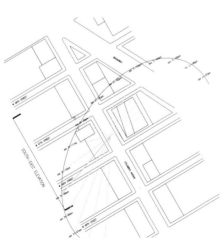

SUMMER JUN 21

PLAN

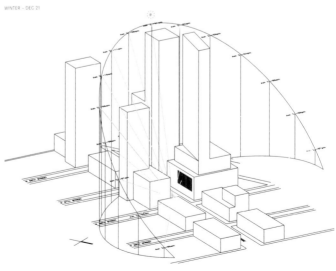

NORTHEAST VIEW

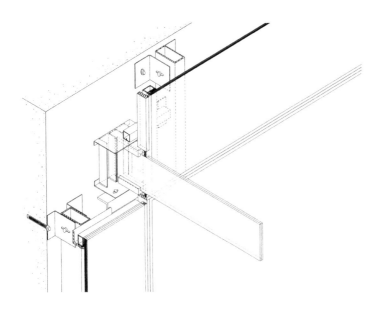

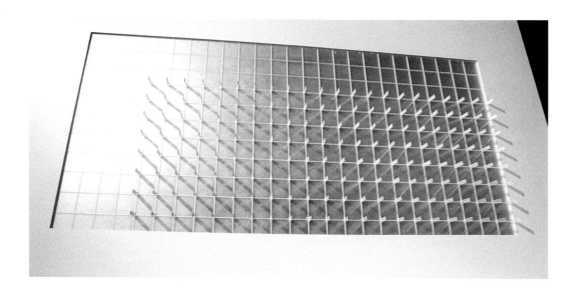

The installation is comprised of two main elements: a flat plane of glass panels arranged in a grid, which can be described as a glass screen, and 216 dichroic glass fins that emerge perpendicularly from this glass screen. The screen consists of chemically strengthened laminated panels that are both textured and semi-reflective, secured to a simple steel substructure. This glass screen reflects and diffuses the light conditions in the sky, from leaden snow-clouds to the brilliant blue of New York's brightest days, while also acting as a semi-opaque surface, not only to hide the structure and wall behind but also to register the light phenomena created by the fins. The dichroic coating on the fins is vacuum deposited and laminated within them. The dichroic coating splits the light spectrum, reflecting a range of colors from one half of the spectrum while transmitting the remaining half. When seen from the north, the field ranges from pale green to indigo; when seen from the south it ranges from gold/green to magenta.

< For ease of installation and to achieve the flattest plane possible for the diffused glass screen, the substructure supporting the panels and fins was designed to be adjustable to account for the imperfections of the concrete wall behind. An aluminum and steel square tube structure is attached with structural silicone to the glass panels while a bracket is anchored to the concrete wall with epoxy bedded bolts. A pin attaches the bracket to the perforated tube for adjustability. The fins are butted and mechanically attached with silicone to an aluminum profile fixed in a steel bracket.

⌐ This study model, made of glass elements, was used to examine the installation's effect on direct sunlight through the day and seasons, thereby determining the diffusion and reflectivity of the glass screen, the glass fins and the choice of dichroic coating.

∨ The panels of the glass screen were installed and adjusted before the fins were slipped between the panels into the aluminum guide rail.

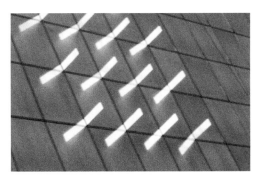

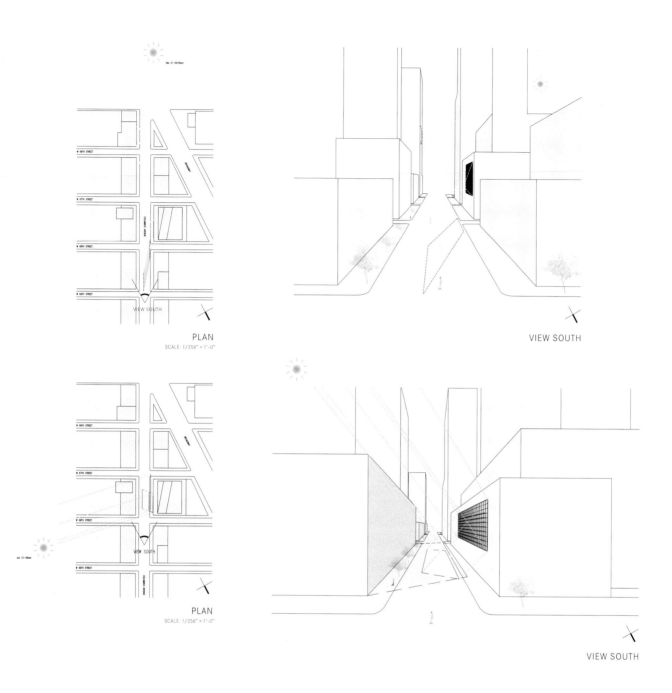

PLAN
SCALE: 1/256" = 1'-0"

VIEW SOUTH

PLAN
SCALE: 1/256" = 1'-0"

VIEW SOUTH

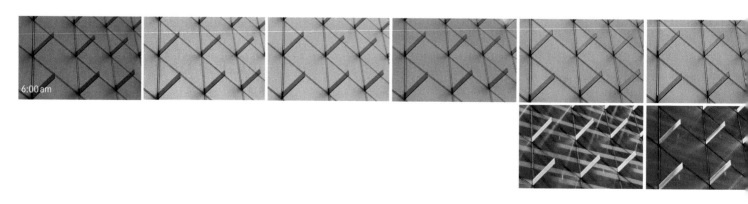

6:00 am

INDIRECT LIGHT
⌐ The sun hits the surrounding buildings at different angles depending on the time of day and season. The diagram illustrates the behavior of the indirect light.

DIRECT LIGHT
< The whole field acts as a huge reflector projecting direct and indirect light onto the street, bringing light into the shadow cast by the building across the street. The summer solstice finds the most direct sun reaching the glass screen and also the deepest shadows cast by the surrounding buildings. Exposed to direct light the diffused mirror of the glass screen reflects its most direct projection into those shadows.

INDIRECT LIGHT
∧ Once the sun passes west of the axis of Columbus Avenue, the installation is in its shaded condition for the remainder of the day. Reflections from other buildings now come into play, particularly in the summer when the sun arches above the highrise buildings. Here, a reflection that has bounced up Columbus Avenue projects an image of those reflective buildings onto the glass screen. The light activates the fins, and the glass screen reflects enough light to illuminate the street shadows.

∟ This single detail of the installation is seen at 30-minute intervals through the course of a clear December day.

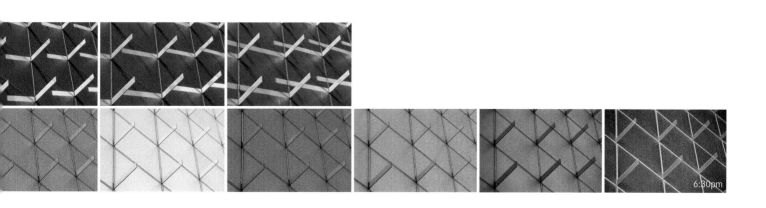

6:30pm

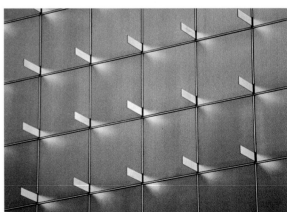

⌐ ∧ Activated by the low winter sun at noon, which at that time is nearly oblique to the fins, and by sunlight reflected off other buildings, these views from the south and north present the wall at its most complex.

<< In these overcast yet bright conditions the installation is at its most subdued. The square grid of the glass screen is broken only by the varying linear perspective of the fins.

On a sunny winter day, as seen above when the sun is almost due south of the installation's east-facing plane, the Dichroic Light Field is at its most complex, presenting a number of light phenomena at one time, which, additionally, are perceived differently by pedestrians walking north or south on Columbus Avenue. The sun is at its lowest and most oblique angle relative to the glass screen, and consequently almost faces the fins head on. Sunlight bouncing off glass buildings to the south also reaches the installation at different angles to the sun's direct light, resulting in a field of cross-hatched reflections, transmissions, and cast shadows.

Direct and reflected sunlight activates the dichroic coating of the laminated glass fins from more than one angle. Thus each fin reflects more than one bar of yellow light and correspondingly transmits more than one bar of magenta light. The linear quality of these reflected and transmitted colors is balanced by the pattern of small vertical dashes projected by the polished edges of the fin ends. Categorizing multiple levels of pattern and their relationships to the viewer does not take into account the installation's intimate relationship to time passing: this installation acts much like a sun clock, yet, instead of casting shadows to track the arch of the sun, it practically dissolves itself as an object, and embodies the qualities of daily and seasonal light. Beyond identifying the daily and seasonal responses to light, pedestrians walking past are brought into the moment by the Dichroic Light Field's constant spatial mutability.

PERISCOPIC VIEWING ROOM

Salt Lake City | Utah | 2001–

∧ View of the mountains.

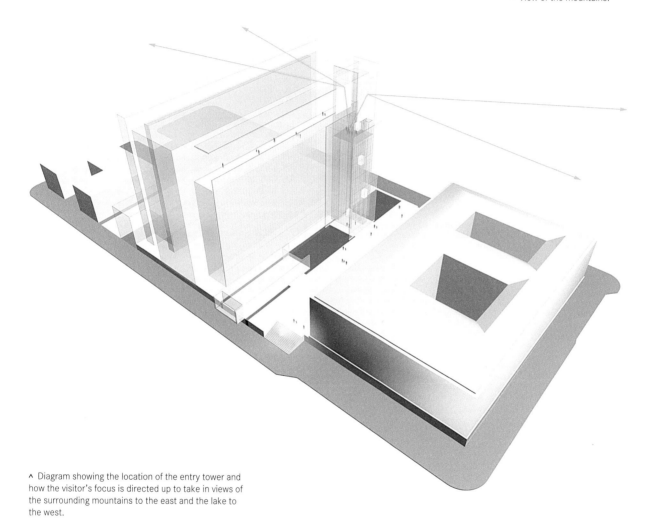

∧ Diagram showing the location of the entry tower and
how the visitor's focus is directed up to take in views of
the surrounding mountains to the east and the lake to
the west.

In the design for an artwork for the new Frank E. Moss
Federal Courthouse organized by the General Services
Administration, James Carpenter Design Associates focused on the courthouse's location at the city's civic core.
Salt Lake City is situated within a bowl created by mountain ranges to the east, north, and south, with the open
plain of the Great Salt Lake to the west. The city's immediate relationship to this extraordinary natural setting
is the prime motivation for the installation. Marking the
presence of the new Courthouse, the architect, Thomas
Phifer & Partners, designed an entry tower that extends
high above the adjacent roof elevations. Carpenter's

team saw the entry tower as a site for an expansive work
that would allow the simultaneous experience of the
urban and natural environment.

At the top of the entry tower, there is an open room,
accessible to the public by glass elevators, which run up
from the plaza level. The east and west walls of the tower
extend upwards, and a series of reflective micro-louvers
that act as periscopic devices bring the mountain range
and Great Salt Lake into the viewers' angle of vision. The
surrounding landscape is projected onto and compressed
on the wall surfaces of the room, creating a juxtaposition
of opposing views.

∧ The views of the mountains are periscopically compressed by the micro-louvers.

⌐ Model demonstrating the micro-louvers' ability to selectively capture distant views.

> Rendering showing the mirage-like quality of the view of the mountains captured by the micro-louvers.

⌐ Cross section of the entry tower showing views brought in from above the courthouse structure.

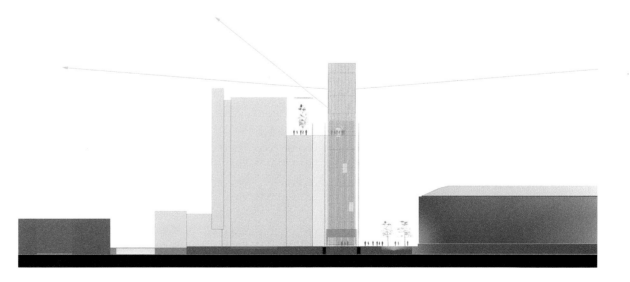

STRUCTURAL GLASS PRISMS

Indianapolis | Indiana | 1985–1987

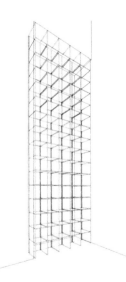

∧ The window's manipulations of light phenomena don't interfere with the congregants' view out.

⌐ This simple structural glass system allows uninterrupted views of the surrounding countryside.

< Diagram of the 32 foot (9.75m) monolithic vertical glass lengths and short horizontal lengths.

<< The upward slanting bars of light convey images of clouds and birds while the downward bars convey the movement of trees and leaves.

Structural Glass Prisms, a dichroic window installation, was designed to bring the outside in, illuminating the Christian Theological Seminary's Sweeney Chapel's large space. In keeping with the spare rigor of Edward Larrabee Barnes' design, the client's brief for the chapel was to create a clear glass window encouraging the meditative observation of nature outside the chapel.

James Carpenter Design Associates' simple design unifies structure and effect. The vertical 32 foot (9.75m) high glass blades are stabilized with horizontal panels of dichroic glass, creating an all-glass structure free from any steel that might obscure the view. JCDA conducted studies of the sun's penetration to ensure the Structural Glass Prisms' ability to project light into the baptistry niche on the opposite wall at around noon every day.

The exterior of the installation is composed of lengths of monolithic glass identical to the interior vertical lengths. This design made both the fabrication and installation more efficient. Using structural silicone, the exterior and interior vertical lengths were attached, after which the short horizontal bracing sections were structurally siliconed to the interior lengths, leaving a space against the outer glass to allow warm air to rise up the length of the glass preventing condensation.

∧ The depth of the window is extended to match that of the building's walls. The resulting depth is divided into a grid of cubes.

> Mock-up demonstrating the Structural Glass Prisms' principles.

∨ Sequence from film showing light projections from morning to afternoon.

The installation is divided into an equal number of squares consisting of horizontal dichroic glass sections stabilizing vertical clear monolithic glass lengths. The coatings on this interstitial grid maintain the transparency of the glass while generating an array of image reflections projected onto the wall.

Two reflected and two transmitted bands of color each project onto the chancel wall, combining to form patterns of remarkable complexity that constantly change in relationship to the sun's position.

The grid-like arrangement of the glass and the use of dichroic glass affects light much in the way that a prism would. Some imagery is projected onto the chapel wall and floor: when direct light from the sun to the dichroic glass is interrupted by the movement of clouds or birds passing across the sky, those shadows are transmitted into the space by the upward slanting bars of light. At the same time, the leaves of adjacent trees, moving in the wind, are visible in the downward slanting bars of blue light, thus creating a superimposition of landscape and sky.

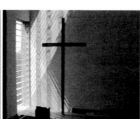

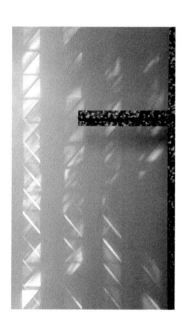

^ The effect of the trees interrupting the light that reaches the window registers as interruptions in the dichroic reflections and transmissions.

LICHTHOF

Berlin | Germany | 1997–1999

^> The façade's slight reflectivity is framed by a less reflective border of glass. The reflectivity visually extends the courtyard into the street.

For the Lichthof, James Carpenter Design Associates designed a curtain wall that would create a layering of imagery to embody the rich architectural history of the Werderstraße. The Lichthof is the primary public space for the German Foreign Office in Berlin. Conceived by the architects, Müller Reimann Architekten, as a light-filled courtyard with a glazed roof and façade onto Werderstraße, it serves as an orientation space for the public that enters the building, and as a symbolic space through which the public sees into the workings of the institution and the institution sees out to the public it is serving. The design of the façade and roof needed to manage the ecology of such a large volume, primarily light and temperature, and to establish a visual experience commensurate with the Foreign Office's desire for safety, transparency, and a bright day-lit space.

The design of the roof and façade exploits the functional needs of the courtyard to create an almost tangible experience of space and light. Carpenter's team worked with architects Müller Reimann and with Schlaich, Bergermann und Partner to achieve the most minimal yet blast-resistant structure for the curtain wall design and with Matthias Schuler of Transsolar to manage the ecology of the atrium. With an almost pure expanse of colorless glass, treated with reflective coatings, which selectively reflect thermal radiation, a subtle play of reflection and transmission balances the corresponding qualities of mirror and window.

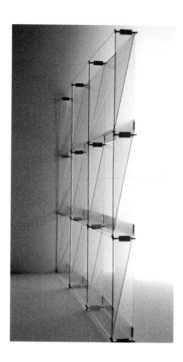

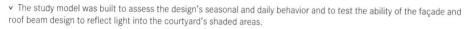

^ Engineered by Schlaich Bergermann und Partner this detail shows an example of the cast stainless steel arms that are cantilevered to both support the horizontal cables and the dichroic glass bands that reflect and project light onto the façade.

∨ The study model was built to assess the design's seasonal and daily behavior and to test the ability of the façade and roof beam design to reflect light into the courtyard's shaded areas.

^ This early study model was for an open façade design capable of allowing smoke extraction in the case of fire. This concept was later exchanged in favor of a sealed design that would allow control over the courtyard's temperature and humidity.

The Lichthof faces north, and therefore the back of the space is in shadow throughout the year. The desire to address this lack of light had to be balanced with a need to control the temperature of a space whose roof is entirely covered in glass. To illuminate the back of the courtyard, the deep roof beams were faced with aluminum specular reflectors angled to be most effective on the darkest days of the year. A lenticular cable truss roof design spanning the main beams was chosen to let in the maximum of light. The roof, angled toward the inside of the façade, has a reflective coating that also brightens the darkest part of the courtyard.

The dichroic bands of glass appear to float inside or outside depending on the light conditions, reflecting blue light towards that source and transmitting yellow light away from it. Often, the balance of light inside and outside is so close that various parts of the dichroic bands are blue while others are yellow. When looking at the wall from within, one sees the reflected image of the sky behind superimposed on the view of the sky in front.

^ View at dusk showing the effects of the façade's semi-transparent glass.

< The maximum balance in light intensity between the interior courtyard and the outside allows for the best views through the glass and the subtlest play of reflections on the façade.

MOIRÉ STAIR TOWER

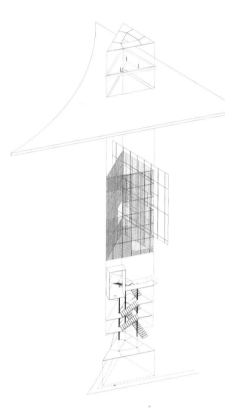

Located along the Rhine River in Bonn, Germany, the new Deutsche Post headquarters is divided into two distinct elements: the 240m (787 foot) high office tower and the three story base building with a grid shell roof. James Carpenter Design Associates was asked to design a stair tower for the vertical circulation volume integrated inside the base building. Carpenter and his team, led by senior designer Richard Kress, focused on the relationship of the stair to the river and adjoining park, to create a stair that would act as a viewing platform, layering views of the surrounding landscape with their reflections as well as the optical effects created by the patterns and their reflections.

The new Deutsche Post headquarters was designed by Murphy Jahn Architects as a signature building for the German Post Office, signifying its shift from national enterprise to global service corporation. Similarly to the German Foreign Ministry in Berlin, the client wished for a maximum of transparency to demonstrate the company's way of doing business and openness to new ideas.

Almost every element of the stair tower is glass, including the etched laminated glass stairs and landings. The laminated glass wall panels contain the screen pattern. The rectangular pattern is a 100% mirror facing out and bright blue facing in. From outside, the effect of a vast field of small equally spaced mirrors pixelate the landscape and sky. Positioned on a landing between levels are two viewing balconies that present unmediated views out, one facing the river, the other facing the Deutsche Post's tower. At night, lights illuminate the two platforms and the stair's translucent glass treads, transforming the tower into a glowing blue lantern visible from the Rhine and surrounding landscape.

∧ Detail showing custom machined point attachment system.

↗ Early study of the screen pattern's exterior and interior colors.

< Exploded axonometric showing the skylight, roof, curtain wall, glass volume, stair, and glass floor.

> View of model looking down from above the volume.

↘ View looking down from the top of the stairs.

∨ Section showing the location of the Moiré Glass Tower in the Deutsche Post base building.

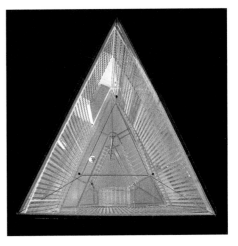

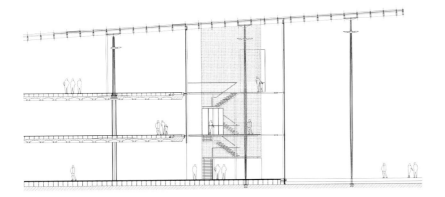

The Moiré Stair Tower's original concept as a scrim-like tower was further developed, through material studies and models. Color was explored to clearly identify the stair tower's critical circulation function. JCDA studied the possibilities of using a mirror pattern facing outwards to capture the surrounding landscape and intense blue on the reverse to suggest both the sky and the landscape in the surface.

Once this concept proved successful, a model was made to test the types of glass to be used. Then different types of diffused glass were explored for their ability to create a luminous volume. In the finished project, the design team chose transparent glass applying a mirror pattern on the exterior and blue on the reverse. This allowed the triangular plan's capacity to generate layers of reflection to achieve the desired luminosity.

LIGHT PORTAL

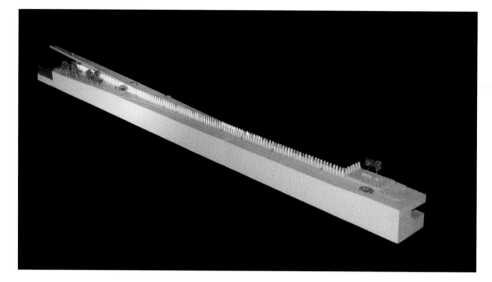 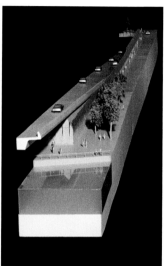

^ ↗ The model shows one side of the portal framing the highway's transition from bridge to tunnel.

> > ↗ Plan of downtown Boston showing where the highway goes from bridge to tunnel, creating a 200 x 700 foot (61 x 213 m) rectangular obstruction in the city's fabric. The Light Portal was designed to highlight the pedestrian paths that circumnavigate the rectangle, passing below the highway at the bridge end and above the highway at the tunnel end, restoring access to the river.

The Light Portal was designed to organize and mark the pedestrian paths that circumnavigate the rectangle of the Boston Central Artery site, passing below the highway at the bridge end and above the highway at the tunnel end, restoring access to the river.

As part of Boston's "Big Dig," the Central Artery Tunnel Authority awarded JCDA with the challenge of producing an environmental artwork that would make the underpass and roadway transition at the Charles River's edge created by the new Leonard P. Zakim Bunker Hill Bridge safer, distinct, and navigable. Instead of designing a single object, the scale of the infrastructure suggested linking the Frederick Law Olmstead Storrow Memorial Embankment to the new Paul Revere Park and other parks along Boston Harbor. The site also needed an acoustical barrier, a means of directing pedestrians, access to the river, and illumination.

JCDA's team discovered that delineating the transitions from bridge to tunnel could define a path for pedestrians and a threshold for drivers. This threshold could match

the site's significance as an important access point to the city.

The necessity for a concrete acoustic barrier where the road dips below grade and the need to visually connect both sides of the barrier to link the experience of pedestrian and driver led the team to design a series of fins such as those mounted between opposing lanes to avoid glare from oncoming car headlights. Retroreflective film, a material used in highway applications is activated by drivers at night and would glow in the low-light areas under the bridge, guiding pedestrians through the space. Retroreflective film uses a printed micro-prism whose cubic or tetrahedral geometry reflects light back to its source. When seen obliquely, the fins combine into a continuous illuminated line, framing the bridge-to-tunnel transition. JCDA remodeled the acoustic barrier in a set of pyramidal forms that echoed the bent aluminum forms of the fins themselves, and found suppliers to anodize the fins using a dye that matched the film.

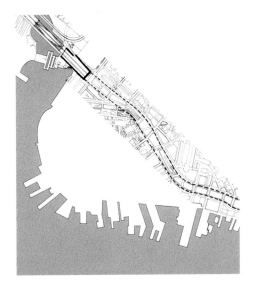

> View at the tunnel of the anodized aluminum fins with their reflective elements.

⌄ Full scale mock-up.

LUMINOUS GLASS BRIDGE

Marin County | California | 1987

< The diffused glass bridge deck captures the images reflected off the river's surface.

∨ This cross section of the bridge shows the minimal profile achieved by the use of post-tensioned glass planks and thin trusses inspired by the engineering work of Robert Le Ricolais.

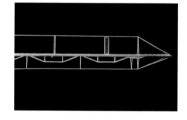

The Luminous Glass Bridge was designed as a conceptual project for a private client. The idea was to create a structure that would push the limits of glass and bridge design, demonstrating the potential of glass as a structural material.

Crossing a small river in California, the bridge proposal aimed to translate the idea of a bridge into an experience of the river itself, engaging the users with an immediate connection to their environment. The bridge design guides the pedestrians along (or against) the river's current. The sun hitting the surface of the water reflects the image of the moving water up onto the underside of the translucent glass deck, allowing for the observation of the river through its own projected image.

The glass platform, a series of post-tensioned glass planks, is supported at each end by two abutments cantilevered from opposite shores approximately 80 foot (24m) from each other. Serving as a means of access, these abutments extend over the river and are spanned by the glass platform. Proceeding out along the abutment-gangway, the pedestrian is re-oriented to travel up or down the translucent glass planks' projection of the river surface. Positioned along the length of the bridge are three slightly reflective panels of glass that also serve as an integral part of the structure. These panels pivot as one moves along the walkway, capturing and layering various reflective views of the environs. Through the use of glass the bridge merges its structural and optical functions.

< View showing the bridge with its three pivoting glass panels that reflect the landscape.

ᵛ Plan view of the bridge shows the opposing abutments which are the sole supports of the bridge's glass deck.

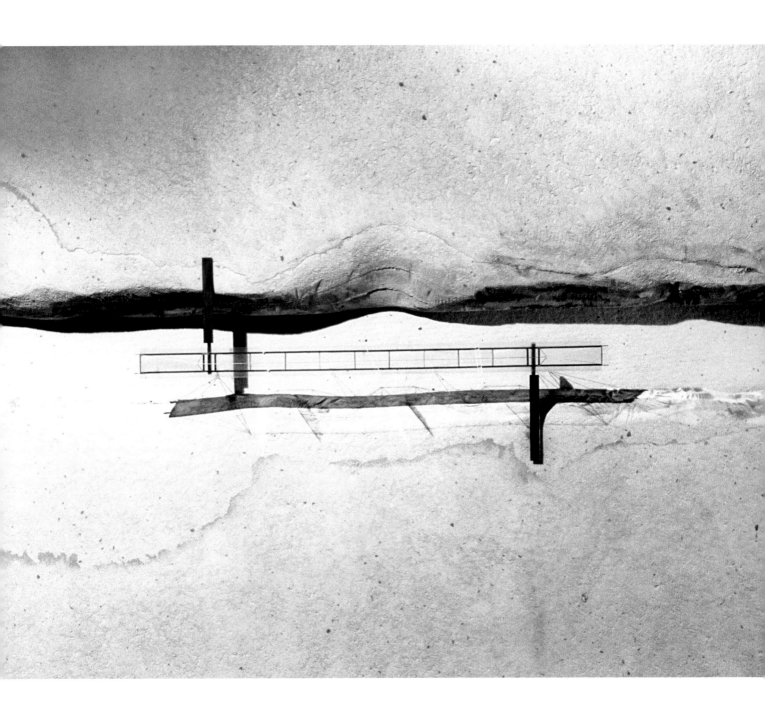

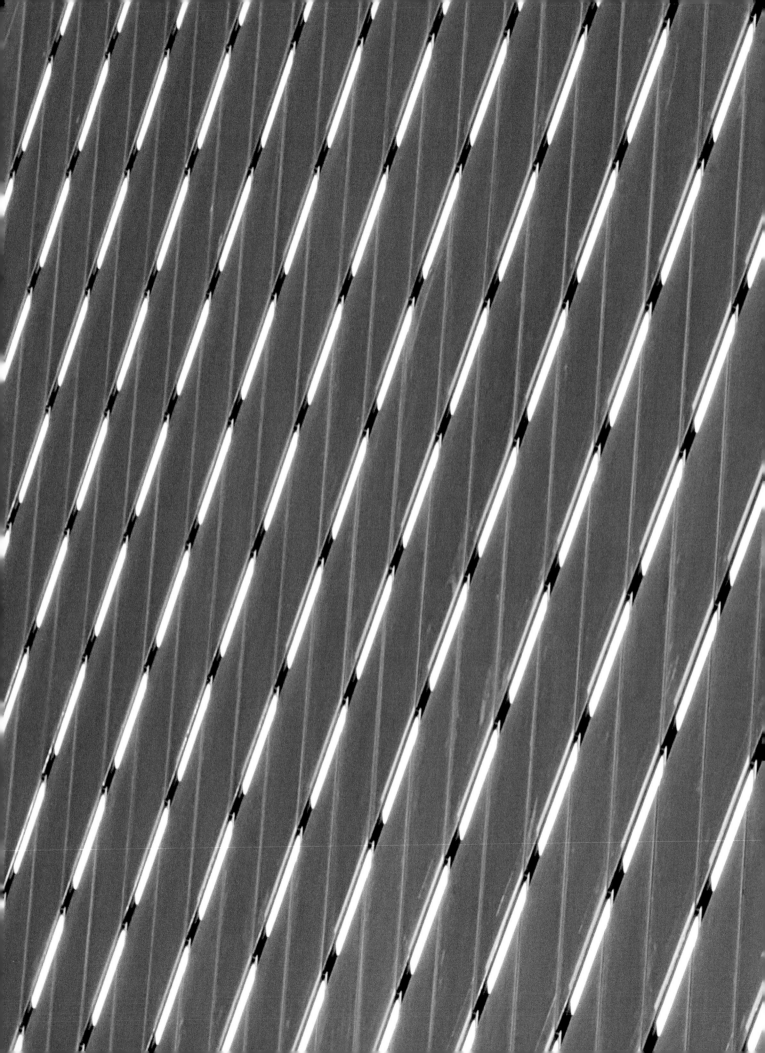

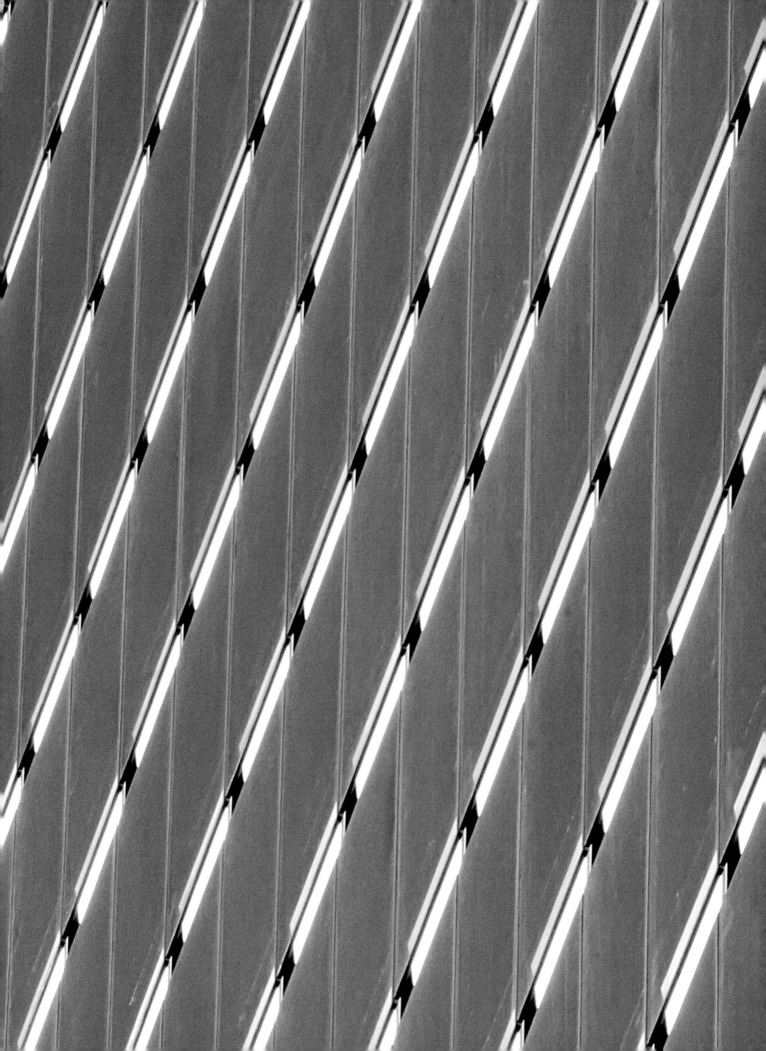

II CONSTRUCTIONS

«You must reckon with the practice of language, and then you will be able to see its logic... you must not forget that a language game is, so to speak, something unforeseeable. I mean that it is without foundations; it is not reasonable (or unreasonable). It is there—like our life.»

LUDWIG WITTGENSTEIN | *On Certainty*

With *7 World Trade Center,* Carpenter has pushed the sculptural horizon of art objects towards significant integration into the complex processes of large building construction. He positively affected the development of quality in this building by paying close attention to its process of production, through his active collaboration with other architects, engineers, and artists.

I will first look at this project as a three-dimensional development of the planar works discussed in Section I, by addressing the impact of Carpenter's work on the legacy of architectural minimalism. Then, I will present *7 WTC* as a case study of research and development applied to the steel and glass components of a significant architectural realization.

With *Periscope Window* and *Dichroic Light Field* Carpenter addressed the architectural notions of window and wall by deploying his knowledge of glass to transform the perceptual operations of these building components. The project for *7 WTC* raises a more radical challenge: that of the architectural object's possible disappearance, notwithstanding its permanent location in a site. The notion of object fulfills the conditions of architecture's consistent materiality, casting it as a thing that could remain forever in its place. Carpenter's contribution consists in challenging architecture's aspirations for the stability of its objects to enter into a kind of black hole of monumental consciousness.

Insofar as *7 WTC* is the first act of reconstruction of a building complex destroyed by a traumatic event that has had repercussions on a global scale, it is an architectural object fated to acquire the status of monument. Yet Carpenter's work has explored this condition of apparent inevitability by confronting the modernist legacy of architectural minimalism, with its various conceptual exclusions between a building's materiality and its urban situation.

Mies van der Rohe's work offers the most direct way to address the notion of architectural object through the tangible rigor of its constructive order. The minimalism of his work consists in making an entire edifice appear as neutral sign. Mies introjects the contradictory poles of attraction and repulsion between monument and city through his architecture's formal silence. However, the spaces of his glass buildings turn out to be not as accessible as the freedom that their transparency promises.

In New York City's *Seagram Building*, Mies moved architecture's tectonic expression towards the perimeter of the edifice, by making the bronze posts external to the curtain wall into catalysts for the reality of the building's mass. The 'I' columns attached to the glass surface create alternating perceptions when viewed from different angles, oscillating between frontal transparency and lateral opacity. Only the symmetrical extension of the plaza's horizontal plane into the transparent lobby anchors the building's thick skin on the travertine slab that reaches Park Avenue.

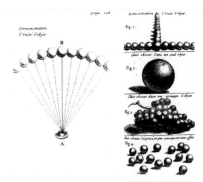

The role of this building's detailing in the establishment of its muted form is matched by an enigmatic absence of images, manifesting Mies's intellectual indifference towards the flux of urban perceptions. While the consistency of the *Seagram Building* restitutes these perceptions as perverse duplications, it also obliges the city to look at itself in a mirror that speaks of architecture's will to dominate its own constructive conditions, silencing all else.

SURFACES

As opposed to Mies's accomplishment of monumental stillness and reflective silence through a declaration of transparency, Carpenter's work explores the supposed correspondence between architecture's constructive content and the technology of its formal expression. If the discipline of architecture were to confine its field of practice to the composition of visual objects with stable properties, it would isolate its involvement with the construction of the visual field before acknowledging its conditions of urban visibility.

Carpenter reduces the materiality of glass to an absolute minimum, yet he finalizes this reduction in support of the perception of its spatial effects in the urban field. He exploits the architectural notion of curtain wall, countering the repression of its potential richness formulated by a modernist aesthetic of glass. His use of steel and glass absorbs the city within the building's mass by introducing the role of time through a precise control of effects produced by direct and incidental light.

For *7 WTC,* low-iron glass was selected to create the most transparent envelope possible. The building's structural columns are inset from the acute vertical edges of the tower to allow its silhouette to de-materialize. Yet transparency in itself is not the only relevant pursuit of this project. The curtain wall design also takes on the conceptual challenge of emanating light from within the surface of the building's skin and merging the building itself with the sky.

The thermal glass units partially overlap the spandrels of the office floors, allowing the spandrel units to capture light and project it through and onto the rear of the overlapping glass. To further the building's luminosity, the curving spandrels are fabricated in a textured stainless steel. Horizontal cuts in the curtain wall thus expose glows of color fields reflected on the stainless steel, enhancing the building's urban orientation in relation to different hours of the day and qualities of atmospheric light. This montage of transparent glass and opaque steel stresses the non-coincidence between tectonic means and their architectural ends. The building's vertical field of glass is crossed by dynamic tensions and disturbances, escaping the perceptual conditions of a conventional architectural object.

Carpenter controls the sculptural logics of the building by revealing how layers of light and shadow constitute its tight and regular enclosure, while transforming both its material consistency (heavy/light) and the definition of its boundaries (inside/outside).

Light does not operate in this building in accordance with purely optical parameters, but becomes itself an object of tectonic perception, yet one that is freed from the laws of gravity or support. This diacritical approach to tectonics posits a paradoxical equivalence between the gravity of two million square feet of office space and the materiality of light, by introducing a conceptual oscillation between them, through the exact properties of individual details.

At *7 WTC,* a suspended cube of light introduces a conspicuous link between the glistening volume enclosed by the curtain wall and the relative opacity of the mass at its base. This link establishes complex relationships between the curtain wall whose horizontal layers extend it into the sky and other elements such as podium and lobby, through contrasting images that express the temporality of an open whole, in analogy with cinematic montage. Cinematic montage also constructs a concurrence of different actions through lights and shadows that unfold into a narrative whole, notwithstanding the film's cuts and splices.

While the curtain wall of *WTC 7* fabricates natural light from the depth of its surface, different kinds of light are also reflected by and spill through the tight alternating rhythm of vertical panels that wraps the building's podium with a double layered grille of triangular steel profiles. The texture of these layered steel panels delineates the building's parallelogram perimeter not by marking its limits as a stable object, but as a luminescent porous barrier that redefines the necessity of enclosure. This surface texture constitutes the street level architectural expression of *7 WTC,* recasting the representation of its support systems into an interplay of shimmering refractions.

During the day, the outside screen's variously oriented reflective prismatic wires, program the contextual light while blocking containing huge electrical transformers. The screen's daytime reflectivity transforms into nighttime emanations from within its thickness, in which motion-sensitive LED lighting also tracks the paths of pedestrians. This aspect of optical surveillance introduced by a camera-recognition system gives to the podium an unusual quality of alertness which, complemented by the breathing air flow emanating from the transformers behind the grilles, renders it disquietingly alive.

The podium's perimeter, consecrated to architectural sense, folds into an interior that emphasizes the emptiness of a serene ceremonial entrance comprised between two very different glass walls. The shallow and angled space of the lobby is framed by two other works, resulting respectively from Carpenter's long-standing collaboration with the engineer Jörg Schlaich and his more recent encounter

with the artist Jenny Holzer. A very transparent cable glass wall on the street enclosure and a translucent acid-etched glass wall behind the reception desk mark a unique threshold in the entry
sequence of the building, conceptually suspending it between engineering technology and art form.
In the case of Carpenter's collaboration with Schlaich, a newly patented lamination technology
transforms the tensile wall into an effective protection against bomb blasts, pushing the fragility of
glass to the limit of absorbing brute force. The productive pairing of Schlaich's pursuit of minimal
lightweight structures and Carpenter's inclusion of other aspects of glass has a precedent. At the
Time Warner Building, also in New York City, Carpenter and Schlaich captured, between the two
angled glass walls of its atrium, the conflicting spectacle of car traffic along the axis of 59th Street
and the performances taking place at "Jazz@Lincoln Center." They accomplished this by doubling
the effects of transparency and reflection which appear to belong to a single surface, when seen
from both the urban outside and the theatrical inside.
In the case of Carpenter's collaboration at *7 WTC* with Holzer, the oblique approach to an etched,
double walled glass volume behind the reception desk diffuses the legibility of a scrolling memorial
statement, pushing glass to produce different quantities of information in relation to the direction-
ality of its perception. This line of work has a precedent in Holzer's probes about the sources and
destinations of messages in our society of the spectacle through architectural intelligibility. In a celebrated installation at Mies's *Neue Nationalgalerie* in Berlin, she brought attention to the con-
strained frontality of the building's empty plaza, by applying lines of scrolling text under the floating
ceiling slab, perpendicularly to the secondary rhythm of the mullions, on the building façade.

As much as I have presented *7 WTC's* curtain wall, podium, and entry sequence as parts in relative
isolation, their design development and implementation have taken place within the temporal
unfolding of a complex process. At this point, I would like to inscribe the considerations about the
two glass walls—realized with Schlaich and Holzer—in the context of a wider set of collaborations,
rather than framing them exclusively in terms of their physical and spatial properties.
The architectural firm Skidmore, Owings & Merrill, with David Childs, who has been in charge of the
overall design and execution of *7 WTC,* also provided the framework for managing its "fast track" realization. The temporal parameters of this schedule provisionally defined the terms of collaboration between
the practices of architects, engineers, and artists, through which Carpenter has navigated over the

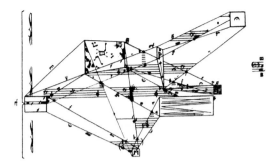

course of the past four years. With his work, he has actively participated in the convergence of diverse actors responsible for the finished quality of the three parts of the building discussed above. Carpenter's career has moved between the disciplinary fields of architecture, engineering, and art and their communicative conventions. His effectiveness within the complex web of relationships that define the boundaries of these fields relies on a sense of precise timing in the deployment of his technical competence. The construction of study models and full-scale mock-ups has marked key moments in an accelerated sequence of actions whose sense has taken shape while they were happening. Although the results have an apparent affinity with sculptures, they are divested of the longing for mastery and control. They have been enmeshed with the evolution of Carpenter's work of design, testing, interface with other actors, fabrication, and installation. He has leveraged the fast track schedule of the project into a set of opportunities for reassessing design priorities, and has used the uneven duration of different phases of the work towards the achievement of higher standards than those typically associated with commercial architecture.

In this context, rather than providing art work, Carpenter's role has been that of introducing a coefficient of art into the building. The difference here is between what was expected at the beginning of the overall process, yet did not happen, and what happened without it having been predefined. This description of his creative initiatives influences the notion of time itself as a regular sequence of intervals: a fast-track construction does not just correspond with a musical "prestissimo." On the one side Carpenter's work has managed to construct its internal consistency; on the other, it has been repeatedly perceived from the other members of the collaborative team (owner, managers, architects, engineers, artists, technicians) in terms of its appropriateness for an immediate utilization.

STAVES

In this part of the book, a matrix of images becomes the diagrammatic concept for the interpretation of the project. The matrix emphasizes the relation between the unfolding of time and the availability of documentation about the process that has led to the completion of *7 WTC*. Time in this case is not only addressed as a property of an object's visibility, as in the projects of Section I, but also as a measure of relevant aspects of Carpenter's work within the overall process of construction.

The project's drawings and photographs are organized in three horizontal bands that dispose the design development of the curtain wall, podium, and entry sequence of this building along a timeline that extends through several pages. The matrix presents moments of material accumulations along each of these parallel bands, layering onto them an uneven perception of multiple times and durations. The "beginning" of the diagram marks Carpenter's involvement in the project, which starts as the building's foundations are poured. The clusters of images of his work are interspersed with other images of the progress of the building's concrete and steel structures.

Through this timeline, the diagram of *7 WTC* suggests a radical reassessment of architecture's romantic illusions of purity and control, which would portray the process of design development of a building in analogy with the notion of musical composition. This analogy is inadequate: classical music can be played again and again, with minor interpretive variations of accent, speed, and coloratura from its score, while architectural execution happens only once, in a given site and at a specific time. Architecture's single performance imposes a particular intensity on the relationship between design techniques and their execution, since an architect's efforts will remain on the building site as a fact, with no possibility for encores.

This project suggests that a better analogy may be found in contemporary music, which has challenged the linguistic parallelism of form and content of the classical harmonic order. The pursuit of musical indeterminacy by such composers as Sylvano Bussotti strategically uses notation as a clue for future aural matrices, expanding the conceptual gap between a score and its realization. This score's draftmanship opens up music to the irruption of chance within its compositional system, by promoting circumstantial intersections in the course of its performance.

Instead of the layout of a conventional pentagram, lines and signs drawn at conflicting angles set up an interplay between known and unknown figures. Music is the outcome of concurrent performances, which belong to different conceptions of instrumental execution. Some properties of future interpretations are made visible, yet the three-dimensional aspect of this notation may also conceal other possibilitiess, conceptually located in a deeper space, behind that which is visible on the printed page. The ambiguous spatiality of such a score challenges classical notation, by establishing new musical conventions through the layering of individual performances.

This compositional strategy throws the players back on their interpretive resources, and promotes the possibility for a redistribution of roles between composers, conductors, and members of an orchestra. A score's execution becomes more similar to the unique occurrence of architecture. The participants to a specific event may develop new forms of practice by choosing different instruments or adjusting their sounds to specific locations, or moments. A performance is the outcome of unforseeable interpretive margins established among players, rather than the re-enactment of an orchestra's hierarchical subordination to the cult of composers and star soloists.

7 WORLD TRADE CENTER

New York | New York | 2002–2006

< Rendering showing base and extruded volume with lobby opening onto the new park.

ⅴ Section and axonometric drawings showing 7 World Trade Center in its downtown context.

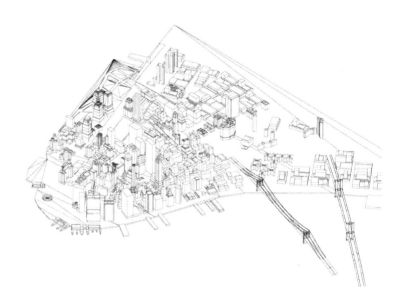

7 World Trade Center was the third building to collapse on September 11, 2001, and is the first building to be rebuilt. Designed by David Childs of Skidmore, Owings & Merrill, the new building is comprised of 42 floors of office space set above eight floors of electrical transformers in large concrete vaults at street level. James Carpenter Design Associates was asked to collaborate with Skidmore Owings Merrill on the design of the building's curtain wall, the base of the building containing the electrical transformers, and the building's lobby.

The new master plan reflected the radically altered context of the site. Previously accessible only from the World Trade Center's podium, four stories above street level, the building, at street level, was a granite cube dominated by industrial louvers venting the electrical transformers that

feed lower Manhattan. With the loss of the World Trade Center's raised podium, the new design had to accommodate the transformers while responding to a public and urban presence at street level.

The concept for the new design was to create a parallelogram in plan, a result of SOM's desire to extend Greenwich Street into the World Trade Center site, extruding it into a 60 story high prism. Grounding the single extruded parallelogram is the solid concrete base volume upon which the glass tower sits. The design team proposed to conceptually lock the base and tower with a third interior volume of light, a "locking block" whose form becomes most apparent at night. This use of light as a design rationale posited the idea that from the podium to the curtain wall, light should appear to be emanating from the building itself.

^ View during construction with the World Trade Center site in the foreground.

< The intersecting grids found at the site led to the parallelogram shape of the tower.

7 WTC's curtain wall evolved from the developer's desire to create an energy efficient yet cost-effective façade. Early ideas involved a double façade and thinner floor plates but due to city codes, construction trades, and cost, this was not possible. Instead 5 x 12 foot (1.5 x 3.7m) double glazed panels with low-iron lites and special transparent coatings achieved an efficient and low-cost solution.
> Full-scale working model of the curtain wall to test the lapped glass unit and the reflecting performance of the spandrel daylight reflector.

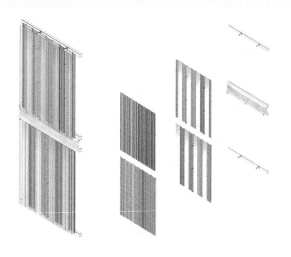

MAY 2002

7 WTC groundbreaking;
JCDA: 1st briefing by SOM

JUN 02

JCDA introduction of shiplap curtain
wall and podium double screen

↘ Early studies for the spandrel panel unit to test the effects of various
reflectors and specular metals

↘ View of concrete transformer vaults during construction.

The Con-Edison electrical transformers at the base of the building require 50% unobstructed
access to the outside air to be adequately ventilated. JCDA saw this limitation as an
opportunity to explore transparency, reflection, and refraction using stainless steel wire.
JCDA proposed a double screen of two layers of triangular wire, experimenting with the
angle of these wires and the possibilities of inserting light between the layers.

< Early detail mock-up of the prismatic screen and supporting structure.
∨ Layout studies of screens, early model, and analytical fluid diagrams of airflow
through the screen by Johnson Screens.

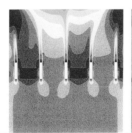

JUL 02

AUG 02

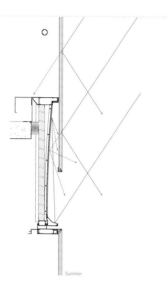

Summer

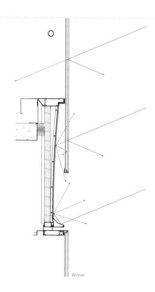

Winter

The success of the colored light in the podium led to programming lighting ideas for the "locking block" and later to the idea of transforming the activity of pedestrians into nighttime emanations of light. At night, the "locking block" is delineated by the illuminated glass ceiling box in the lobby and programmed LEDs within the podium's skin. At dusk, the light shifts from white to a radiant blue, while the podium's internal LED lighting also defines this same volume with blue light. After dusk the blue locking volume is gradually replaced by vertical bands of blue on the podium walls which are triggered by a camera-recognition system that tracks passing pedestrians and signals the LED bars to follow their path.

Activated as the viewer passes by, the prismatic wire screen's appearance alternates between dark and light. < Early model of the wire's nighttime luminosity and daytime light reflection. > Drawings showing sun or ambient light-reflection angles.

SEP 02

JCDA introduction of LED podium lighting scenarios with SOM.

OCT 02

In keeping with the central organizing idea that light should emanate from the building, JCDA with SOM developed a unique "linear lapped" glazing detail in which the vision glass overlaps and floats in front of a curved spandrel panel with a built-in sill reflector. The curved spandrel panel is made of a diffused, reflective stainless steel deeply embossed with a ribbed specular texture that captures both the local light conditions and the light reflected by the blue stainless steel reflector located in the sill of the spandrel. The reflected color and light of the reflector and spandrel panel is continually projected through the lapped section of the glass façade.
< Drawings showing spandrel's redirection of sun's rays; renderings of curtain wall showing blue sill and spandrel's reflection and detailing at corners.

At the entrance through the cable-net wall's perimeter, the stainless steel of the podium folds from the exterior into the lobby. The cable-net wall, measuring 105 x 44 foot (32 x 13.5m), is comprised of highly transparent (low-iron) glass with narrow diameter stainless steel cables and a 12 foot (3.65m) glazed canopy extension.

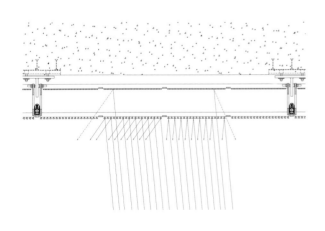

NOV 02

DEC 02

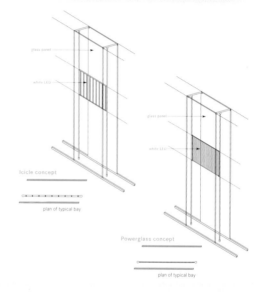

ⅴ Early study for the transparent letters explores the angle response of LED light traveling through various layers of glass.   ＞ Drawings of different lobby wall LED concepts.

glass panel

white LED

Icicle concept

plan of typical bay

glass panel

white LED

Powerglass concept

plan of typical bay

JAN 2003

1st meeting with Holzer on interior lobby wall collaboration.

FEB 03

JCDA & Holzer lobby wall presented to Silverstein.

Both the podium and the curtain wall present a rhythmic interplay of reflection which could be calibrated: in the podium's case by the angle, dimension, frequency and reflectivity of the prismatic wire, and in the curtain wall's case, by the spacing and size of the spandrel's reveal, the color and angle of the blue reflector and the texture and curve of the spandrel reflector.   < v Curtain wall and podium mock-ups compared to confirm their relationship of scale and the quality of light.

JCDA collaborated with Jenny Holzer to develop the concept of floating transparent words traversing the width of the lobby. This concept involved developing LEDs suspended between two layers of diffused glass. This 14 x 65 foot (4.3 x 19.8 m) translucent glass wall was set behind the reception desk parallel to the building's entrance. Jenny Holzer created a memorial statement from quoted texts, letters 5 foot (1.5 m) tall scrolling across the glass volume.

MAR 03

1st (of many) mock-up reviews of curtain wall and podium, Connecticut.

APR 03

JCDA cable-net wall documents completed.

↘ Following each tier of steel, a temporary steel working deck was assembled in place over center core area until the concrete core could be completed.

∨ Detail drawing of cable-net wall fittings.

Given present-day bomb threats, the cable-net entry wall was developed by JCDA, SOM, and Schlaich, Bergermann und Partner as a bomb resistant, energy absorbing wall. Using proprietary lamination technologies, the cable-net is flexible in nature allowing the wall to absorb and dampen the effect of a blast. The glass elements are mechanically restrained by embedded carbon fiber and Kevlar anchors so as to allow movement yet always remain captured, regardless of the forces encountered.

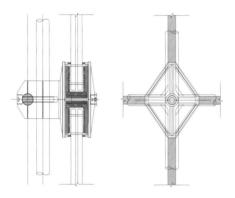

The full scale mock-ups were used to demonstrate their ability to survive wear as well as to explore the exact effects of light as it interacts with the double wire skin. The initial mock-up tested the toughness of the stainless steel wire.

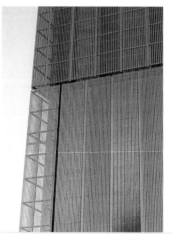

MAY 03   JUN 03   JUL 03   AUG 03

Once the visual success of the curtain wall design was approved, a second full scale mock-up was fabricated. This performance mock-up tested the curtain wall's ease of installation, replacement of panels and ability to withstand seismic and hurricane forces.   > Views of performance mock-up tested the glazing and linear lapping of the spandrel and joints.   ⌄ Detail of overhanging glass panels and spandrel cavity seen at curtain wall's corner.   >⌄ Detail of blue stainless steel reflector and the custom corrugated specular panel reflector.

⌄ Early rendering of tower.

SEP 03

OCT 03

Curtain wall mock-up, Canada, glass coating review

NOV 03

Performance test mock-up of curtain wall at CRL, Miami, Florida.

The performance mock-up tested the possibility of replacing individual panels within a certain amount of time (above) and the torpedo rig for the window washing track system built into the mullion (left). This channel visually separates the insulated window panels from the mullion and adds to the reading of the curtain wall's delicate attachment to the tower.

⌄ White LED mounted on glass with foil conducting tape.
↘ Early mock-up of LED; RGB LED suspended on vertical wire strand.

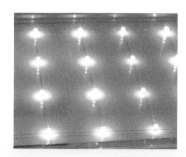

The stainless steel screen panels are made of cold drawn equilateral prismatic wires orientated vertically and resistance welded in a specified pattern and angle of rotation. Welded to a 5 x 14 foot x 10 inch (1,524 x 4,267 x 254mm) stainless steel sub frame, the front screen prismatic wires have 1/2inch (13mm) cross-sectional faces that are highly polished,

while the inner screen's prismatic wires have 1/4inch (6mm) cross-sectional faces that are glass-bead-blasted to diffuse and scatter light. The two wire sizes possess complementary light-reflecting properties and reduce the moiré (bifurcating) effect generally created by two layers of parallel lines.

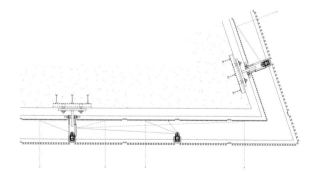
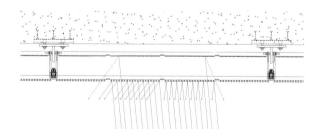

DEC 03

JAN 2004   FEB 04   MAR 04

CURTAIN WALL INSTALLATION: 1. As one floor is completed the stack joints for the succeeding panels are prepared.

At night, the reflections of the scrolling letters will be visible on the adjacent interior wall, floor, and ceiling surfaces. As a lobby wall, this artwork is also designed to provide the elevator core with blast protection.

ᵛ Rendered video explores the scale of text and quality of motion in the lobby environment.

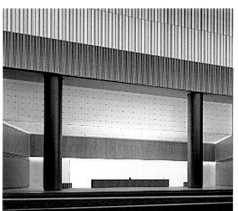  

ᵛ Detail of plan showing the LED fixture located between the two layers of the screen.

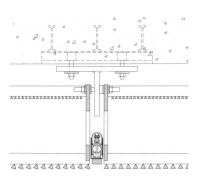

APR 04   MAY 04   JUN 04   JUL 04

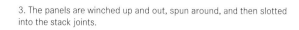

2. The panels are laid out on dollies face up with their stack joints for the next floor facing outward.

3. The panels are winched up and out, spun around, and then slotted into the stack joints.

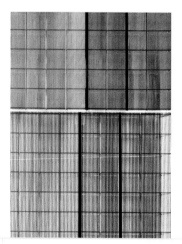

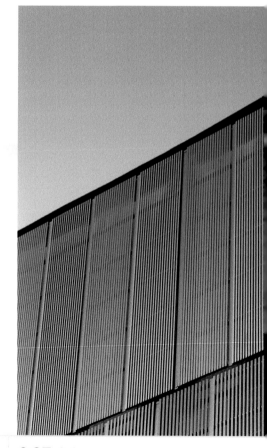

AUG 04

SEP 04

Cable-net wall and canopy review at Gartner in Germany.

OCT 04

LED podium mock-up review, Connecticut.

4. Lastly, the panels are bolted in place.

∨ View of cable-net anchorages to the concrete vault structure.

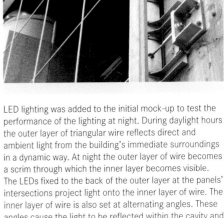

< White LED light (above) was tested for the regular night conditions while blue LED light (below) was tested for the blue "locking block".

LED lighting was added to the initial mock-up to test the performance of the lighting at night. During daylight hours the outer layer of triangular wire reflects direct and ambient light from the building's immediate surroundings in a dynamic way. At night the outer layer of wire becomes a scrim through which the inner layer becomes visible. The LEDs fixed to the back of the outer layer at the panels' intersections project light onto the inner layer of wire. The inner layer of wire is also set at alternating angles. These angles cause the light to be reflected within the cavity and projected back out through the outer wire, amplifying the glowing quality of the light visible on the inner wire's glass-bead-blasted surface and again visually superceding any view into and through the transformer vaults.

NOV 04   DEC 04

> Curtain wall during installation.

ˇ Automated welding of stainless steel prismatic wire to a ladder sub-frame at Johnson Screens.   ˇˇ Finished units stacked at Johnson Screens. The rotated face of each group of prisms reflects opposing sources of light, often resulting in a dark and light pattern.   > Installation of glass panels for the lobby wall.

JAN 2005   FEB 05   MAR 05   APR 05   MAY 05   JUN 05

ᵛ View of lobby wall from rear, before rear glass is installed.   > Testing LED lettering on lobby wall.

> Podium during installation of steel screens.

JUL 05   AUG 05   SEP 05   OCT 05   NOV 05   DEC 05

^ View of canopy and cable net from outside.

↗ View of the cable net and interior illuminated volume that is activated to create the "locking block".

↗↗ From the elevator core, the LED text is seen in reverse.

∨ View showing the LED light as its reflections scroll across the lobby's surfaces.

JAN 2006

7 WTC near completion

TIME WARNER BUILDING

New York | New York | 1999–2004

∧ View down 59th Street at sunrise.

↗ Jazz@Lincoln Center's Allen Room uses the double cable-net wall's transparency as a backdrop.

James Carpenter Design Associates, working with SOM, developed a complete scheme for the atrium enclosure at the Time Warner building on Columbus Circle in New York. The complex is comprised of two towers separated by an east facing atrium, measuring approximately 150 foot high by 85 foot wide by 90 foot deep, and subdivided horizontally into the main public entry and retail at the lower levels and the performance lobby for Jazz@Lincoln Center at the upper level.

To match the scale of the volume and the urban street grid, JCDA conceived the largest cable-net wall ever built: the width of the wall matches the width of 59th Street, visually extending it into the building. The most radical element was the hanging of two cable-net walls from a single inclined truss. The outer 150 foot (45.7m) high cable-net wall is anchored to the top chord of this inclined truss while the inner cable-net wall is anchored to the lower chord of the truss. The exterior cable-net wall presents a unified highly transparent plane of glass, while the interior inclined cable-net acoustically isolates Jazz@Lincoln Center from unwanted sound, while maintaining complete transparency to the street below, providing the audience with direct views of Central Park and 59th Street. The low-iron glass also allows uninterrupted views into the retail space as well as into Jazz@Lincoln Center's lobby performance space. The initial proposal incorporated a glass roof design with an integrated shading system that would allow views of the sky at night but this element was not adopted.

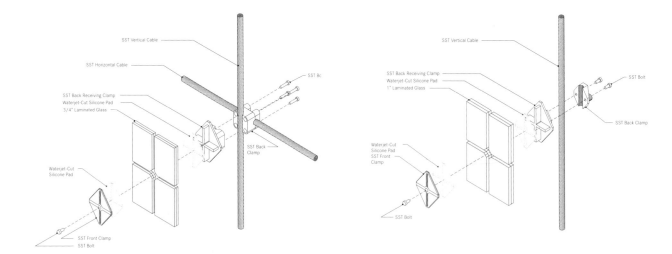

SST Vertical Cable
SST Horizontal Cable
SST Bc
SST Back Receiving Clamp
Waterjet-Cut Silicone Pad
3/4" Laminated Glass
SST Back
Clamp
Waterjet-Cut
Silicone Pad
SST Front Clamp
SST Bolt

SST Vertical Cable
SST Back Receiving Clamp
Waterjet-Cut Silicone Pad
1" Laminated Glass
SST Bolt
SST Back Clamp
Waterjet-Cut
Silicone Pad
SST Front
Clamp
SST Bolt

∧ Exploded axonometric of outer cable-net.

↘ Exploded axonometric of inner cable-net.

> Axonometric of double cable-net wall.

∨ View of the cable-net wall at ground level.

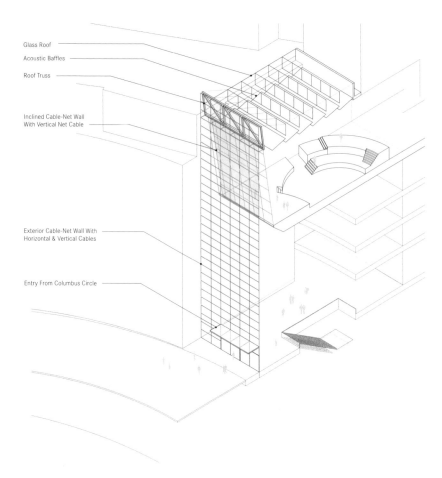

Glass Roof
Acoustic Baffles
Roof Truss
Inclined Cable-Net Wall
With Vertical Net Cable
Exterior Cable-Net Wall With
Horizontal & Vertical Cables
Entry From Columbus Circle

JCDA, working with Schlaich, Bergermann und Partner, faced particular challenges due to the desire for the most unimpeded plane of glass possible, the sheer scale and mass of glass, the incline of the inner wall, and the resulting forces the cables would have to support. The resulting design for the inner wall used only vertical cables anchored to the inner chord of the large truss. The glass was used structurally to handle horizontal loads.

The outer cable-net wall's cables are tensioned and secured from the basement, through the retail space's entrance structure, to the truss, while the inner cable-net wall's cables are attached to the truss and descend to springs attached to the Jazz@Lincoln Center's floor beams. The springs allow for the deflection and additional live load forces applied to the cables caused by crowds in Jazz@Lincoln Center.

∧ View from inside the lobby entrance looking up between the two cable-net walls.

∨ View of the entire wall at night with a performance underway in the Jazz space.

LENS CEILING

∧ Details of the final installation.

> Installation near completion.

Commissioned to design the ceiling for the Special Procee-dings Courtroom of the new Sandra Day O'Connor Federal Courthouse in Phoenix, JCDA proposed the Lens Ceiling as not only a public artwork, but also a part of the archi-tecture, a building almost entirely built of glass designed by Richard Meier and Partners. The piece sought to enhance the theatrical nature of the space while acting as a multi-functional building component: an acoustic barrier; a day and artificial lighting system; and support for the fire and life safety system. The delicate, suspended cable struc-ture describes a spherical form intersecting a horizontal plane, as if a bubble of air were resting gently on a surface of water. The spherical area of glass is diffused, creating a luminous sculptural element that captures the sky and the shifting shadows of the building's structure without dis-tracting attention from the proceedings in the courtroom.

^ View of the architectural model. The Special Proceedings Courtroom can be seen through the public atrium structure.

⌐ View of the Special Proceedings Courtroom.

The Lens Ceiling made of various laminated glass panels provides a thermal, acoustic, and dust barrier for the courtroom space. The central lens area acts as a precise diffuser for the artificial lighting mounted at the top of the drum, while the clear horizontal perimeter ring of glass visually frames the lens and allows views of the sky from the public viewing gallery. JCDA also designed an innovative solution for the mandated sprinkler system, fabricating the sprinklers out of stainless steel and integrating them as working members of the cable-net tension structure.

The structure was engineered by the New York office of Ove Arup & Partners. Seismic events were considered and a complete three-dimensional finite element model of the structure was built to assist in analysis. Movements within the structure due to changes in temperature are accommodated at each glass panel, and even after an accidental panel breakage, nothing can fall because the laminated glass is mechanically attached to the structure through a very thick interlayer normally used in hurricane-prone areas.

< The clear perimeter glass frames the diffuse rolled-glass lens. The public mezzanine has direct views into the courtroom and views through the clear glass of the sky above.

v Exploded axonometric of the cable-net, glass and courtroom structure.

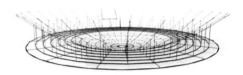

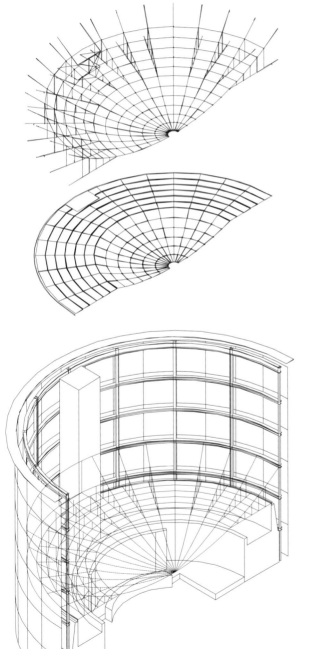

^^^ Model testing the installation method.

^^ Early rendering of the suspension system.

^ Inspection of the laminated glass testing.

RETRACTING SCREEN

Dallas | Texas | 1993

∧ The human form visible on the screen is a diffused shadow cast onto the back of the screen from the private dining room.

↗ This photograph taken from the private space catches the screen retracting into the floor.

↘ Plan detail showing location of the screen.

The screen for this private residence was imagined as capable of dividing the space while conveying images, both reflected and transmitted. Designed by Richard Meier & Partners, the residence included a gallery space for the display of the client's extensive collection of modern and contemporary art. The dining room was conceived as a flexible space adjoining the gallery which would also function as an ancillary reception area for the gallery. It was suggested by the architect that JCDA propose a design for a glass screen between the two spaces.

The concept for the screen grew from the variety of light conditions in the spaces surrounding the screen and the public/private quality of the space. The bright lighting on the art objects in the gallery, the subtle low light of the private space, and daylight playing in different ways on either side of the screen led to the idea of a mutable surface that could have many varying appearances.

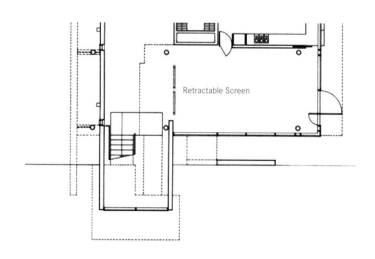

Retractable Screen

∨ View of the screen from the gallery at night. The screen is reflecting artworks on the wall opposite as well as the reflection of those artworks in the polished granite floor.

∧ Sequence of studies exploring levels of transmission and reflection.

> ⁊ Installation of glass screen.

> Drawing showing the structure and parts that allow the operable screen to descend into and emerge from the basement.

∨ Impact tests of hard and soft projectiles to establish the structural integrity of the post-tensioned glass concept.

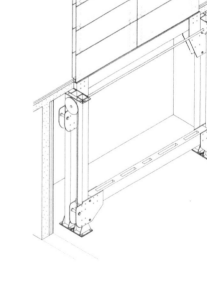

A simple observation in the studio of the superimposition of glass with a subtle low-iron colorless reflective coating, and acid-etched glass, grew into the concept of a screen made of two separate layers of glass. The tension between the crisp, subtle reflection in the coated glass, and the outline of objects beyond the screen diffused by the acid-etched glass, became the subject of a careful exploration of the integration of material, structure, and light. The acid-etched glass sheet faces the dining area to capture the glow of low lighting, while the coated glass faces the gallery to reflect the illuminated objects on display. The challenge was to have a minimum of structure interfering with the glass itself. This was solved by incorporating a beam below the level of the floor from which the two separated layers of glass are cantilevered. The two panels are spaced apart and capped with a stainless steel plate to allow stainless steel rods to pass up between them to compress the glass panels, thereby transforming the panels into the structure itself.

JCDA developed the structure and mechanism for the screen wall. The structure consists of a pair of beams that travel up and down the two vertical columns. As one beam goes up the other goes down by means of geared chains that connect them. One beam supports the screen while the other acts as a counterbalance enabling a small electric motor to move the 2,000 lb (907kg) wall up and down.

^ View from the gallery of the screen retracting.

GLASS TUBE FIELD

London | United Kingdom | 1998–2003

^ Early rendering of the glass tubes showing the concept of visually extending the depth of the threshold with both the glass tube struts and their reflections in the cable-net wall.

↘ Early sectional rendering of the atrium threshold established by the field of struts.

James Carpenter Design Associates was asked to develop concept ideas to enclose the wedge-shaped atrium of the Tower Place Development in London, designed by Foster and Partners. Following on JCDA's work at the German Foreign Ministry in Berlin, JCDA suggested a cable-net wall which was to be suspended from the atrium roof, floating 5 m (16 foot) off the floor. Tensioned horizontal cables would be tied into the flanking buildings' floor plates, thereby supporting the glass. To reduce the overall horizontal cable length and its deflection, a field of intermittent struts was placed evenly at 10 m (32 foot) to carry the load back to the columns supporting the roof.

JCDA noticed that, as in the Berlin Lichthof project, light could reach the atrium's dark corners by applying reflective levels to the transparency of the façade's interior glass surface. Furthermore, the typical metal horizontal struts needed to prop the horizontal cable-net wall could be replaced by a horizontal field of laminated structural glass cylinders whose reflections in the façade would extend and enhance the experience of traversing the atrium threshold.

> The concept for this design was first conceived in 1988 for the Southern California Gas Company Headquarters in Los Angeles, CA.

Ensuring the safety of the annealed glass tubes, which would break into large sharp pieces in case of failure, was of primary importance. JCDA initially assumed that it would be relatively straightforward to laminate two tubes together, post-tensioned with a central stainless steel rod anchored to two stainless steel end caps. The post-tensioning of the glass cylinder reduced its bending and allowed the glass to take positive loads induced by wind forces, while the stainless steel cable would resist the negative or suction forces also caused by the wind. Experiments quickly proved that there were several serious problems with this, the most immediate one being that any dimensional change in the laminating resin either de-laminated or broke the assembly due to the materials' expansion or contraction during curing. The solution was to divide the outer tube into two lengths allowing it a greater margin of movement, but the resin lamination proved difficult to do cleanly without spillage. The design of the building was suspended at this point, which allowed JCDA to carry out a series of small experiments with will-

ing contractors and institutions in the hope of finding a successful prototype for future use. In 2000 several experiments trying different methods of bonding two tubes were undertaken at the Massachusetts Institute of Technology Materials Sciences Department. This research demonstrated that there is a successful method using an ultraviolet laser to cure the lamination resin in concentric bands, thereby guiding the forces resulting from the cure along and out of the cylinder.

Schott Rohrglas was capable of making the tubes at the length (4m), thickness (about 10mm), and diameter (about 200mm) needed (13 foot x 4/10 inch x 8 inch). JCDA proposed using a stainless steel rod down the center of the tube to post-tension the cylinders, and the engineers calculated that a 10mm diameter rod would be able to comfortably resist the façade's wind loads. The inner tube was laminated with conventional interlayers to a segmented outer tube, each segment half the length and one third of the tube's circumference.

v Sequence of development of glass tubes, from the left to the right.

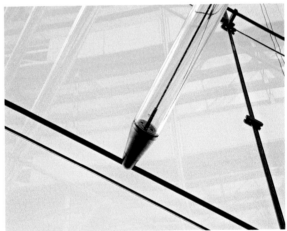

III APPARATUSES

«It was not enough to describe the outline of the reflections on the balcony to render the impression conveyed by that ray of sun... [until] all of a sudden, without our comprehending why, in a word that appears to be totally insignificant we are given access to a speck of a certain kind of higher pleasure—the pleasure of poets—as the only thing we cannot have any doubt about.»

MARCEL PROUST | *Le rayon de soleil sur le balcon*

The horizon of Carpenter's ongoing contribution to a contemporary agenda for architecture can be understood by looking at two types of work. The first is a body of early gallery installations that used short films as their primary medium. The second is a collaboration with the architect Vincent James in which Carpenter effects the project's environmental agenda. As opposed to the temporal proximity of the two projects chosen as paradigms of Section I, these works are more than twenty years apart.

The preceding sections have addressed Carpenter's challenge to the conception of the object in relation to the fields of both sculpture and architecture. Section I introduced the notion of a device that creates a delay in the presumed immediacy of the perception of sculpture. As devices, both *Periscope Window* and *Dichroic Light Field* shift an understanding of window and wall away from that of utilitarian building components, extending their function to encompass the temporal experience of light and perception itself. Section II extended the challenge raised in Section I about the limits of a phenomenological reading of the work to confront the conditions of its visibility in the city, and to address complex processes of professional collaboration in the fast track realization of *7 World Trade Center* in New York. The role of time as a dis-continuous aspect of this work has pointed to the cinematic notion of montage as a way to resolve the historical conflict between sculpture, architecture, and landscape—in an urban or natural context.

To address the apparent paradox of choosing heterogeneous and temporally remote works as paradigms for this section, I will build upon the notions of device and montage, using them to address Carpenter's construction of spatio/temporal thresholds that establish relationships between phenomena of perceptual redundancy and experiences of environmental disorder. Both the film installations of the 1970s and the architectural project for Tulane University three decades later position themselves within environmental flows that reach out beyond their physical limits, by addressing more than one event and making these events perceivable. The temporal and technical conventions that organize the spacing between elements conceived through this framework are affected by these large scale processes, taking on a dynamic role.

Both the film installations and the Tulane project acknowledge different rhythms in the source and destination of the flows that they engage. These rhythms reach a moment in which they can share a space, notwithstanding their internal and mutual gaps. The resulting spaces are constellations converging from remote lines of resonance between motivations and narrative structures that don't belong to a single order.

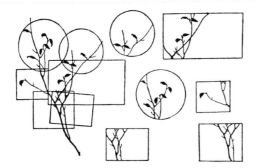

FILM INSTALLATIONS

I consider the five film installations *Confines, Cause, Homing, Koi,* and *Migration* as a representative sample of a comprehensive body of video work, not only because most of them were presented within a short time frame at the same gallery (between 1975 and 1981, at the John Gibson Gallery in New York), but also in light of the relative consistency of their cinematic parameters. All five films take their imagery from natural ecological systems, depicting processes and activities independent from yet parallel to human thought and purpose. The protagonists in Carpenter's films are all animals, whose motivations in different contexts must be inferred by the spectators.

The view point of the camera in these films is from above, and the shots relate the animals to a horizontal fixed frame, irrespective of habitat: ground for the snakes, air for the birds, or water for the fish. Through this insistent horizontality, the footage reveals, amplifies, and focuses the viewers' attention on aspects of the environment that are not dominant, that would otherwise tend to be overlooked while, at the same time, shifting emphasis from what could be a purely visual narrative to the physical quality of the film's temporal interactions with the floor of the gallery.

The subjects of these film installations are, respectively, a snake and a bird displaced on a table, several pigeons flying into a literally framed space, and fish swimming in a pool or passing through water which appears to flow on the gallery's floor. Rather than recreating the relative passivity induced by sitting in the chair of a film theater, these installations prompt a viewer to viscerally engage with the animals' instinctual behaviors, promoting their imaginary spatialization in the darkness of the gallery.

In *Confines*, the film shows a snake positioned on a square surface at whose opposite end are a person's two disembodied arms. Notwithstanding the snake, a pack of cigarettes and a half full glass give clues that the person is calm. The snake slowly moves closer, attracted by the warmth of the person's body temperature, until it wraps itself in slow motion around one of the arms. Through the coincidence between the horizontal plane of this film's shooting and the actual table top on display, this installation addresses a key aspect of the cinematic frame: what matters is that which the camera does not include, outside the physical edges of the table. The unsettling implication is that, while animal and human proceed in the film from wariness to acceptance, other snakes could be on the floor of the gallery, surrounding the viewer as well as the table.

Cause pictures a crow suddenly appearing in the film frame. A dish and a knife confirm that the same ordinary table was used as the surface for the shooting and the projection, yet the unpredictable irruption of the bird into the scene and its intermittent assimilation of food, disrupt associations

with the relatively regulated timing of human meals. In the gallery space, the presence of more black crows, stalking along the room's perimeter, is felt or imagined as if they might pass by in the darkness, attracted by the food on the table. Every time the crow enters the camera's field of vision and has something to eat, what changes is not only its state of need or interest, but the state of the whole situation, encompassing the table and the spectator, and all that lies around them.

Homing shows pigeons flying into a camera's fixed frame, where they are portrayed while gathering, eating, and mating on the ground. The gallery installation projects this film into the middle of an elevated rectangular cage, inhabited by live pigeons. This visual situation cannot be resolved in terms of the spectators' identification of the thickened frame with a theatrical setting. The fact that the pigeons held prisoner by the cage in the gallery are the same as the ones whose image is enlarged to a size similar to that of the spectators, promotes a reversal in the process of perception and self-identification. This psychological oscillation is accompanied by focusing a visitor's attention on the materiality of the film's own grain, foregrounding Carpenter's interests in probing the material consistency of a medium while using it.

As opposed to exploring the implications of the cinematic frame, two other film installations propose strategies for its expansion, by stressing the role of time in the constitution of spatial perceptions. The multiplication of the projected image invests the frame of these two other installations with different perceptions of time, corresponding to their respective emphasis on the inside or outside of the cinematic field.

In *Koi,* the appearance and disappearance of two kinds of colored fish swimming on different levels of a pond filled with water lilies create a random combination of color and shape that contrasts with the formal disposition of the landscape. The red fish are clearly visible in contrast to the lilies' green leaves; the white-and-black ones literally disappear into and out of the mesh of algae below the floating leaves and flowers, moving towards apparently bottomless depths. The transfer of the original footage into nine separate films makes the different parts of their simultaneous projection go out of sync, producing multiple trajectories within the geometric order of the image.

Migration consists of a series of linked frames portraying a very shallow riverbed crossed by the sequential movement of a salmon. The upstream movement of this fish produces traces in the water's surface that create striking effects on the clearly visible gravel riverbed, which is projected onto the gallery's floor. In this installation, the relative disorder introduced by the fish is tempered by the sophisticated setting that follows the salmon's path of movement through separate cameras and projections, establishing a sense of continuity among sequential images. By multiplying each frame by three Carpenter introduces gaps in the fluxes in which the things of nature are borne. The sense of time projected by this installation is also dependent on the expansions and contractions of light due to the weather at the location of the shooting. The projection is full of undulating and sporadic turbulences, mixing the stream's gravel bed, the fish, and the water reflections in the sequential rectangles across the gallery's floor.

In all five of the film installations, a visitor's imaginary engagement with and projection towards animal and/or human bodies in the gallery's space qualitatively change the relations between time and space, whether they belong to the scale of a table as a place of encounter or feeding, or to the scale of an inhabitable frame, a landscape contained in a pool, or a riverbed.

In order to address the way in which Carpenter constructs productive tensions among heterogeneous elements, I will now introduce the notion of apparatus. Rather than pursuing equilibrium, an apparatus enables the co-presence of logics that are remote to each other within the same space, establishing dynamic relationships among the incompatible conditions of experience from which these elements come from.

Looked at through the notion of apparatus, the film installations diverge from a gallery's expected situation, resulting in an overlay of multiple elements which become intelligible from the point of view of a spectator's movements, yet without acquiring a unitary direction or purpose. There are two critical aspects in this process: one, displacing the technical conventions of the established film medium; and two, forming charged settings that exceed the gallery's physical and cultural boundaries.

The convergence of these two aspects of Carpenter's film installations points towards architecture's mandate: to map, frame, and qualitatively transform human encounters between the conditions of a site and the constructive parameters allowing individuals to occupy and use it. Like Carpenter's film installations, architecture has the potential to capture the momentary overlap, interface, and resonance among heterogeneous elements and phenomena engaged at different scales, by establishing their spatial connections and interactions.

TULANE UNIVERSITY

There exists a strong conceptual affinity between the film installations of the 1970s and the way in which Carpenter's current work develops alternatives to the notion of a building as an environmentally self-sufficient object and of its context as a bounded site. With the project for the *Tulane University Student Center* in New Orleans (begun in 1999), Carpenter's work has moved beyond controlling light to ways of affecting other environmental qualities such as temperature and humidity, enriching the range of his materials and technologies, and expanding their application to inhabited spaces.

The project for the *Student Center* was a collaboration with the architect Vincent James. Carpenter's involvement beginning in the early planning phases raises interesting questions about conventional definitions of an architectural design process. The research that Carpenter developed through this collaboration circumvents constraints that are associated with the linear development of a general spatial idea, by focusing instead on elements that modify the building's entry areas, exterior screen walls, and interior ceilings. His work succeeds in redefining the technical challenges that involve these architectural tropes, through the design of precise, limited, yet resonant interventions.

Carpenter, Schuler and James's approach at the *Student Center* is informed by a keen attention for New Orleans's climate, suggesting that the effects induced by environmental situations not only can contribute to the development of a project, but can also constitute its conceptual preconditions. A building located in the humid climate of this alluvial city can regulate uncomfortable conditions by introducing subtle adjustments in the density and permeability of its architectural boundaries. Rather than focusing exclusively on the summer's heat and humidity, the project accomplishes significant modifications of its relations with the environment by giving attention to the temperate climate of the seasons of fall and spring.

This approach expands the comfort zone of an occupant's body temperature through the control of shade and air quality, countering the environmental system of the original 1960s building that had sealed it in an artificially isolated glass bubble with a cold atmosphere, responsive to a polarization of peak climatic conditions. Carpenter's pursuit of subtle adjustments of the building's porous membrane allows instead a layering of enclosures and filters to emerge from the action of localized flows. The moderate equilibrium introduced by this texture of material relationships also suggests to qualify the building's architectural scope as a careful regulation of socio/cultural exchanges.

The *Student Center* is characterized by many kinds of space and time in which activities like reading and socializing elude singular classifications and distribute relative chaos amidst institutional order. In response to this degree of indeterminacy, Carpenter designed a series of architectural apparatuses that address the environmental scope of the project, including shading and enclosure systems, interior fans of different sizes, solar vents and sky lights, and a water wall, each of which establishes a complementary relation with environmental control systems.

Through these considerations, the project undermines the technological assumption that movement of matter in a perfectly efficient system would remain stable until disturbed by some external force. Five architectural apparatuses make clear how the conceptual range of Carpenter's rearrangements of available environmental forces constructs temporally inflected spaces. These apparatuses operate at different moments within the building's daily cycle of activities, in relation to multiple scenarios of occupation and interaction with the environment.

A *Parasol* of perforated steel and operable aluminum louvers sets up a gradation of different angles and widths across its surface and through its layers, operating in analogy with the canopy of a tree. It also acts as an internal/external operator that supports a layered relationship between inside and outside, minimizing the use of air conditioning. As an apparatus, the *Parasol* transforms air from a generic flow (from outside to inside and vice versa) into an agency of dynamic environmental cycles, with a mediating function comparable to the processes of osmosis in the human skin.

Wood and aluminum *Shutters* operate in accordance with seasonal and daily cycles along the west and south edges of the building, animating its skin with a textured surface that includes rotating walls and screens of woven wire mesh, which support climbing plants. Windows complement the louvers' variable density in relation to different uses, adding the possibility of personal adjustments to the localized control of ventilation. These multiple relations among parts consider fluidity not as a rare and particular case of a general condition of solid boundaries, but as a starting point for the design of the building's entire enclosure.

A system of *Small Fans* installed in the ceiling of cafeteria and dining hall provides general air movement through the building. This air movement induces a cooling effect on the occupants, as breezes evaporate water molecules from the surfaces of their skin. Stainless steel actuators and aluminum pivot arms move a light reflective polycarbonate film stretched by steel cables, engaging multiple fluxes of dynamic forces (physical, cognitive, and social) by seasonally varying these rooms' relationships with the outside.

Heat Chimneys are engineered glass cylinders in the second floor ballroom, complemented with tilt-up glazing panels, to be used during the temperate months. Large fan blades push jets of cold air down towards the floor while the sun-heated fritted skylight plates at roof level, causes the hot air to rise up the cylinders by convection. These zones of varying temperature and the passage of air provides a more nuanced appreciation of the room's separation and connection to the outside.

The large *Pendulum Fans* in front of the *Water Wall* push forth air towards the walls' screens, and pull it back, creating a breeze that cools the occupants at the building's entrance. This complex apparatus marks the threshold between the Commons and the inside of the *Student Center*, revealing its climatic variables. The large fans, positioned beneath a translucent scrim that stratifies heat vertically, force air towards a sky-lit vertical steel mesh, on which a waterfall fed by chilled water from the building's air conditioning system condenses the humidity in the air.

By not confusing the conceptual rigor of these five apparatuses with an abstract pursuit of exactitude and technical power, Carpenter effects imperceptible departures from conventional design and engineering logic, establishing them not as a subset of technology but as the very prerequisite for technology's use, through a proliferation of elements that fluctuate around points of controlled turbulence.

DIAGRAMS

The diagrams of this section display a different logic of representation from that of the axonometric drawings and perspectival views in Section I, which analyze the relationships between the sun's path and the devices of *Periscope Window* and *Dichroic Field*. In the case of both the film installations and the *Student Center's* apparatuses, the diagrams stress a flickering luminescent quality as apparitions in the spaces where people are moving, establishing a conceptual relation between their perceptual appearance and disappearance, and the effect of immersion into a film's projected reality.

Yet there is also a qualitative difference between a filmic world of illusions and the diagrams illustrating the two types of work in this section. While a cinematic frame projected onto the screen of a movie theater temporally juxtaposes heterogeneous blocks of images, the diagrams engaging the logics of inclusion and exclusion of Carpenter's installations and apparatuses clearly imply that the forces acting through their physical boundaries extend beyond the spaces in which they are situated.

In contrast to the regular beat in the temporal unfolding of a film's plot, the diagrams point towards the bending of time that results from the animals' circumstantial exposures in the installations, or the operations required by climate in the *Student Center*. In both instances, the diagrams support awareness of the spatial role of framing and the temporal effects of intermittent jolts in their images.

The diagrams present temporal phenomena in which the positions of parts, dimensions, and distances vary in relation to human bodies. They introduce the notion that a perspective view portrays a moment of spatial and temporal awareness connected with the physical and emotional force of events taking place in natural and/or engineered environments. Rather than depicting fixed things, the diagrams highlight subtle yet significant centers of indeterminacy within various processes. The arrows in these diagrams express disturbances and/or changes in the levels of energy. In the case of the installations, they depict animals entering in and exiting from the boundaries established by the films' fixed frames, without relegating these natural events to the role of background for human action. In the case of the *Student Center's* apparatuses, the arrows convey more complex information about the flow of the light, air, and humidity, that are, by their operations, engaged. These arrows, while portraying the flow of physical elements, suggest a relationship with the flow of the occupants themselves.

These arrows bring attention to the mobile position occupied by spectators for whom bodily sensations play a crucial role in establishing relationships with quiet or turbulent flows. They address how order can emerge out of multiple relationships between variable processes that are neither causal nor strictly mechanical. These processes establish a productive relation with some of the manifold logics of animal behaviors and climatic control through the conception of hybrid constructs.

In Carpenter's practice, these hybrid constructs operate by subtly subverting material conventions, thereby relating these conventions to larger flows of energies in a wide texture of phenomena. He takes on challenges raised by technology through research and development of advanced material and engineering solutions, without conforming to utilitarian principles. His works investigate ways in which enfolding, constitutive, and living entities appear within a spatial and temporal frame, without limiting their sense to an environmentally self-conscious distribution of materials and/or harmonious forms.

Carpenter's work discloses the operational potency of fleeting images of real matter, through an ethical dimension that is both embedded in and redefined through his design process. The passage from Proust quoted above points to the interweaving of creativity with the radiance of nature, by virtue of the mental connections it establishes between contingent situations. Carpenter's work both forges and takes apart such connections. It supplants the laws of knowledge proper to natural sciences by pointing towards the unexpected depth of things, while maintaining a keen interest for their possible inhabitation in ways that mediated appearances cannot.

CONFINES

1975–1978

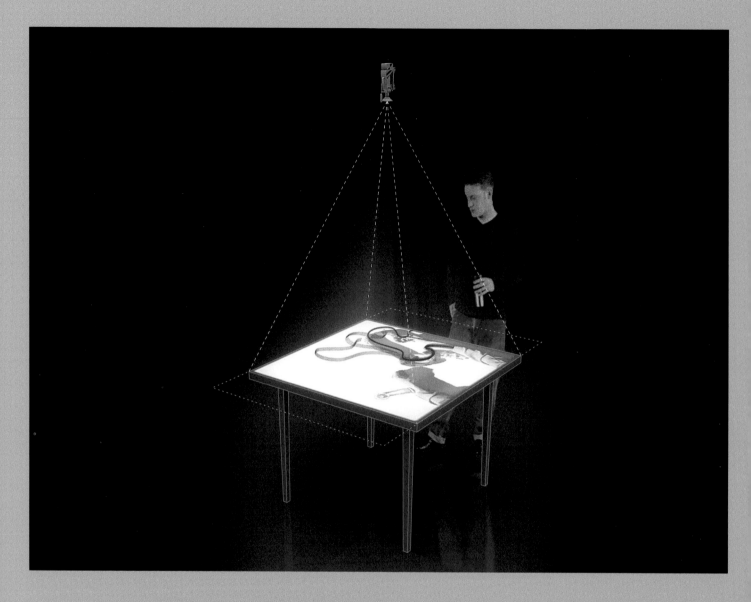

∧ Diagram showing the sequential movement of the various elements observable through the course of the film projection.

∨ Sequence of film stills extracted from the film.

^ Photographs taken during the filming: the artist and snake at the beginning of the sequence; the snake approaching the artist's hand; the final position of all the elements.

< Photograph of installation showing beginning of film sequence projected onto tabletop.

Filmed in 1975 and presented as an installation at the John Gibson Gallery in New York City in 1978, Confines consists of a square table whose surface doubles as a projection screen for a looped single cassette film shot in super 8. The image projected onto the 3 x 3 foot (91 x 91cm) table surface is that of the same table surface at the same scale. The film loop was shot with the camera positioned directly above that table, recording a simple sequence of events; the artist's arms rest on the tabletop, surrounded by ordinary objects: a glass, an ashtray, a cigarette pack, and matches. Across the table is a snake. These elements shift until the cold-blooded reptile, attracted by the body's warmth, wraps itself around one of the hands resting on the table. The title suggests a word play on being confined and the confinement of an image by its frame.

CAUSE

⌐⌐ Photo of the crow during the filming.

⌐ Detail of film still capturing the crow and its shadow as it lands on the table.

∧ Detail of film still of a slice of bread being cut from the loaf.

< Photograph of the installation showing the compressed image of the crow, plate, and bread projected onto the table top.

Filmed in 1975–1976 and shown at the John Gibson Gallery in New York City in 1978, Cause, like Confines, is an installation of a 3 x 3 foot (91 x 91cm) square table whose surface is a projection screen for a looped single cassette film shot in super 8. The image projected onto the table surface is that of the same table surface at the same scale. The film loop was shot with the camera positioned directly above that table recording a simple sequence of events: a plate with a loaf of bread and a knife can be seen on the table; two arms enter the frame and use the knife to cut a slice of bread, then disappear; a crow lands on the table, cautiously approaches the bread, takes the slice off the plate, consumes it, and flies out of the frame. As the bird flies out of the narrow projected frame, the darkness of the gallery space becomes occupied by the crow's virtual presence.

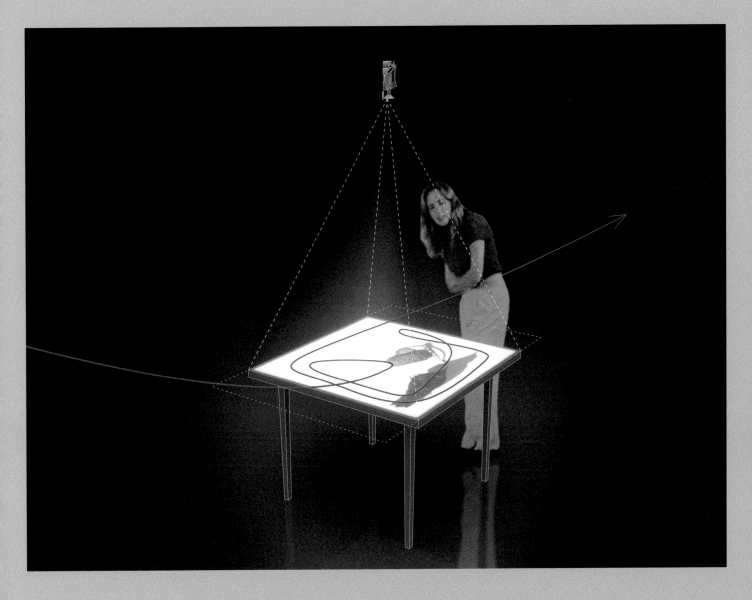

∧ Diagram tracing the movement of the crow in and out of the filmed frame.

∨ Sequence of film stills showing the crow landing on the table and interacting with the loaf of bread.

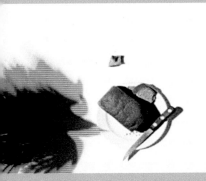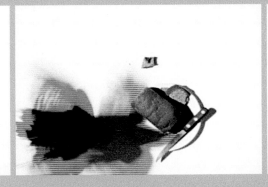

KOI

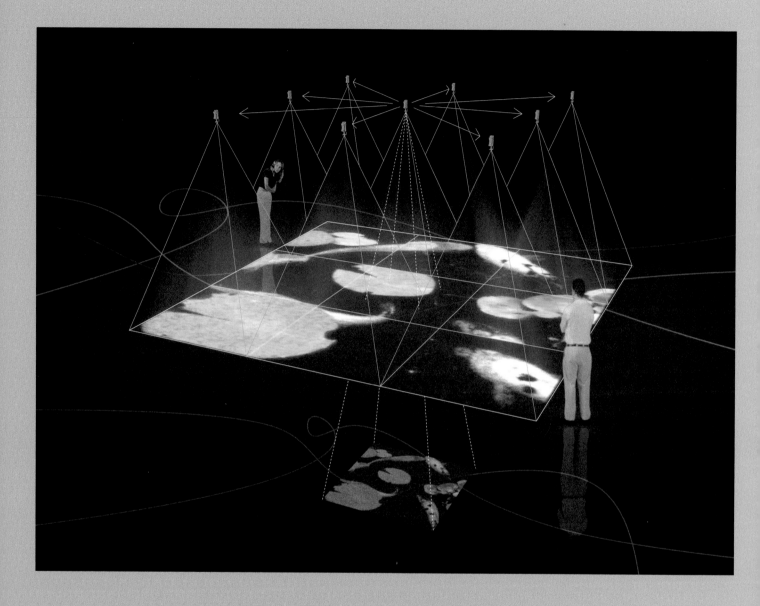

∧ Diagram of Koi, showing the single frame of the film extrapolated into nine frames.

∨ Sequence showing stills from the original film before it was divided into nine frames.

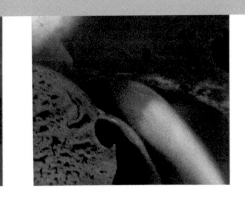

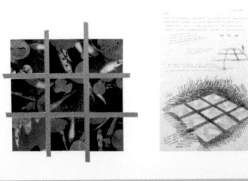

Koi was filmed in 1979–1980 for an installation that, like Cause, features natural elements controlled and transformed by the human idea of nature. The Japanese landscape reflects a culture in which all elements exist in a tightly functional and aesthetic choreography. All aspects of the Japanese garden are orchestrated in one seamless relationship between materiality and mastery. Within the water elements of Japanese gardens, the aesthetic control is brought into relief by the koi, a type of carp that moves freely and unpredictably, presenting dramatically colored and abstract reflections. The koi represent an element of randomness and a spiritual release from the sublime conditions that synthetically attempt to perfect nature.

The installation features Koi in a grid of squares on the gallery's floor. The surface of the koi pond was filmed from above using a fixed camera recording a fixed frame over an extended time, capturing the movement of the fish as they swim below the surface of the pond. Carpenter shot a single film, then extrapolated the original footage into a grid of nine films projected in parallel. The magnification of the fish, the texture of the image, and the grid transform the reality of the koi into a human scale kinetic abstraction.

⌐ Photograph of the koi pond during filming.

∧ Carpenter's sketches for installation.

HOMING

1978 | 1980

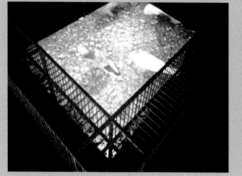

↖ Pigeons in the pigeon coop.

↖ Artist in his pigeon coop.

∧ Photograph of the installation showing the pigeons in their cages.

< Photographs of the installation.

Filmed in 1978 and shown as an installation at the Clocktower Gallery in 1978 and the John Gibson Gallery in 1980, Homing is an installation featuring a group of caged homing pigeons and a film of those same pigeons recorded feeding and mating as they move freely in and out of the cinematic frame. Shot from above using a super 8 camera, the film image is looped and enlarged so that the birds' projected images are 2 to 3 foot (61–91cm) long on the floor. As the birds enter the projected frame they can be seen and heard either feeding or mating within this delineated film image. Encompassing all four sides of the projection is an elevated cage that houses the same pigeons visible in the film. Framing their cinematic versions, the caged birds can be observed reacting to the sounds and images of their recorded selves. The cinematic versions of the pigeons are free yet captured on film while the caged birds are confined but free to react to light and sound. As in Cause, the filmed birds fly in and out of the frame activating by implication the space outside the projected space.

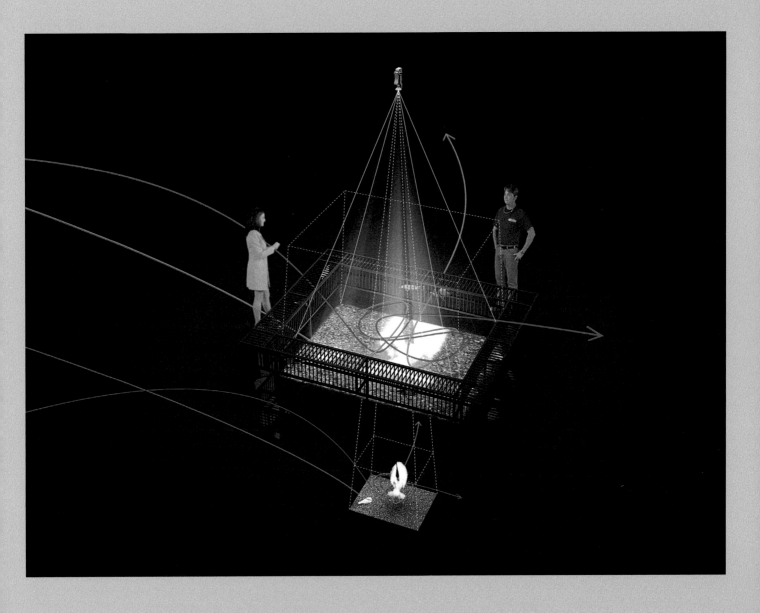

^ Diagram showing the flight and interaction of two pigeons in the film sequence.

ᵛ Sequence of film stills extracted from the film.

MIGRATION

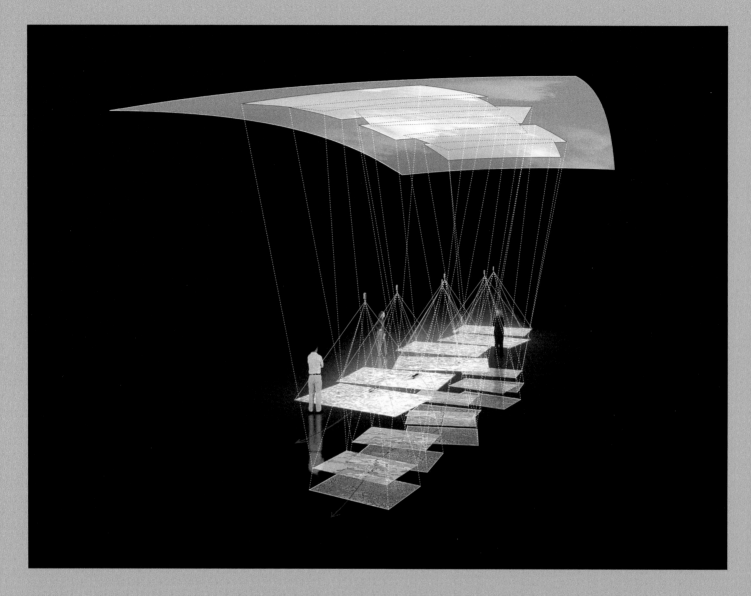

^ Diagram of the installation isolating the various elements of the film image. The top plane represents the projection's reflected surface. The plane below represents the reflective surface of the river with its sky image. The bottom plane represents the gravel bottom of the river. The plane above the projection represents the sky dome being reflected by the water's surface.

v Sequence of film stills extracted from the film: an individual salmon moving through the projected frames.

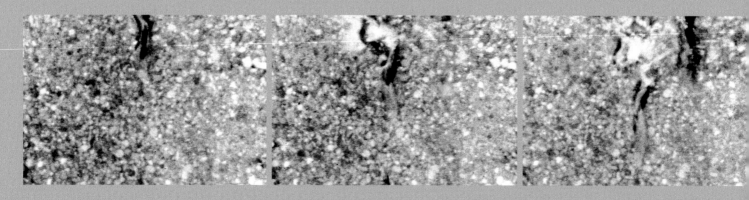

 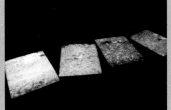 

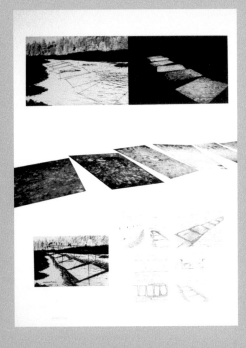 

<^ Installation view at the John Gibson Gallery, New York, New York, 1978.

<< Carpenter's sketches for installation.

Migration is a film installation whose multiple projections of segments of a river were shot on a small shallow stream flowing into Puget Sound. The University of Washington managed the river as a site to experiment with various strains of migratory salmon. Anchored to scaffolding erected over the river, a series of cameras, at 90 degrees to the water, were spaced apart, oriented to follow the flow of water and synchronized, thereby capturing a fractured but accurate record of a 60 foot (18m) segment of the stream. Each of the films was then projected onto the gallery floor at full scale, creating a 60 foot (18m) long installation, reframing the river's flow over the gallery floor. In the gallery, one experienced standing next to the river, which flows across the floor of the space. One could observe the water flow over the gravel bed of the stream and the salmon moving up from one film frame, through a moment of darkness, into the next film frame and so on for a total of nine filmed frames.

In order to heighten the observation of this environmental phenomenon, each film frame was copied to span the duration of three frames so that, during projection, each image was held slightly longer than would normally be the case. By holding the image for a brief instant longer than normal, viewers were able to simultaneously observe the phenomena of migration and the phenomena of light. The image of the sky became clearly visible on the surface of the river and was periodically distorted by the image of the salmon, making visible the spatial compression created by the combination of transparency and reflection.

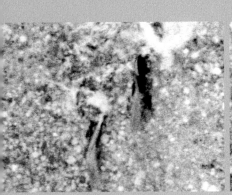 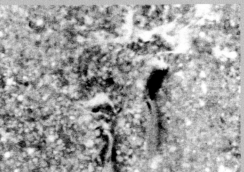 

TULANE UNIVERSITY CENTER

New Orleans | Louisiana | 1999–2006

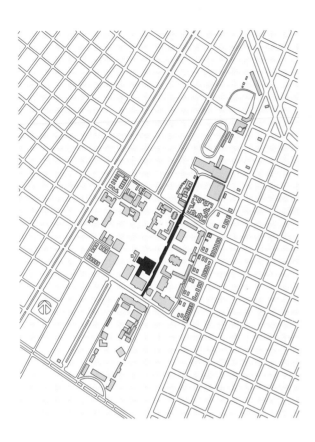

∧ Plan of the campus showing the student center and main circulation routes.

∨ Cross section of the addition showing the interaction of a number of cooling systems, tempering the need for air-conditioning.

> This axonometric diagram shows how the different apparatuses are layered through the building.

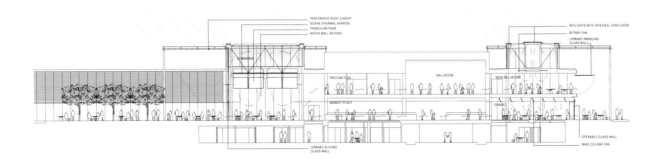

In 1999, James Carpenter Design Associates was approached by Vincent James Associates Architects to collaborate on a large renovation project for the Tulane University Student Center with the common intent of making the program more environmentally sensitive. Over the years, the original 1950s Student Union building had become a sealed box, completely dependent on air-conditioning. Located in New Orleans, known for its hot and humid weather, JCDA and VJAA proposed creating a more open, flexible, and permeable building, inspired by the French Quarter architecture of the region, in particular the use of fans and the extending of the zone between interior and exterior.

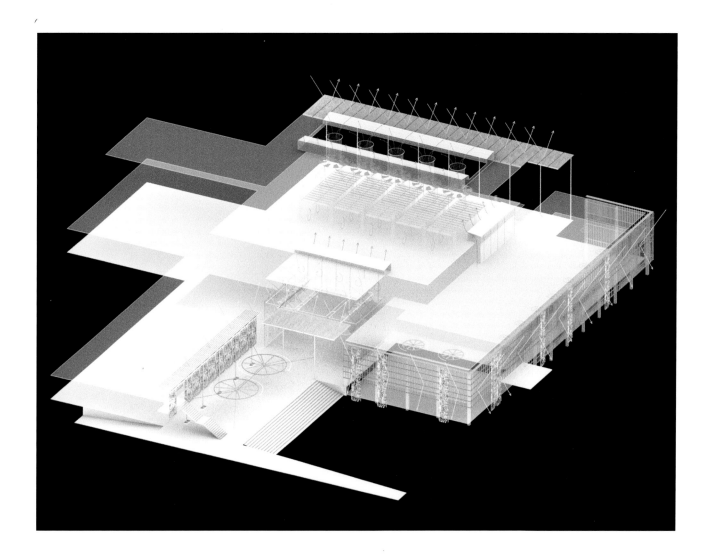

Working with VJAA and Matthias Schuler of Transsolar Climate Engineering, JCDA developed a design that would create shade and increase air movement in the built environment using a series of successive environmental control elements and including a perimeter capable of being either air conditioned or opened to the outside. This series of elements would greatly reduce energy consumption and minimize the conventional use of mechanical HVAC systems. The design comprised a parasol roof structure, automated vertical shutters, a glass enclosed ballroom positioned on the existing roof terrace, large fanning devices, and waterwalls for dehumidification.

The parasol roof structure uses varying densities of perforated metal panels that selectively shield the building from excessive solar gain and enhance natural ventilation by creating hot surfaces to draw air out of the building. On the exterior of the building a mechanized aluminum and wood vertical shutter system wraps around the western and southern façades. This computer controlled screen adjusts automatically during the day and through the seasons, modulating the amount of sunlight into the building, closing to reduce solar gain in the summer and opening to allow light penetrate in the winter. Windows are operable to give personal localized control over natural ventilation. The depth and frequency of each shutter corresponds to the interior programming, becoming wider and more frequent as the interior space becomes more private. In the building's interior the fan systems create significant air movement, providing a cooling effect and assisting in drawing air through the building. Small swinging fans integrated into the ceiling cool the cafeteria and help circulate the air, while large swinging fans in the entrance zone force the warm humid air near the ceiling down over the chilled surface of the waterwall. The cold water causes the humidity in the air to condense and be absorbed into the waterwall, dehumidifying and cooling the air.

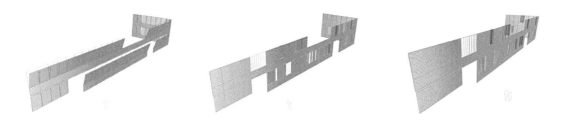

^^ Early façade studies of louver shading concept.

^ Two potential scenarios for the mechanically operated louvers.

LOUVER SHADING CONCEPT

The louver shading concept uses vertical wood and extruded aluminum slats that are operable, changing their density and orientation according to the programmed sequence of space behind. This sequence is designed to balance the need for a determined amount of light while reducing the heat gain associated with direct sunlight entering the building. Though derived from a purely functional problem, the louvers also serve to animate the building skin. The various depths of slats are combined to create a richly textured surface that merges views through the slats with the patterns created by their various orientations and widths. The depth and frequency of the vertical slats respond to the programmed space within. The more public spaces feature shorter and more widely spaced slats allowing a more porous relationship to the outside, while conference or lecture areas feature wider and a greater number of slats, creating a sheltered relationship to the outside.

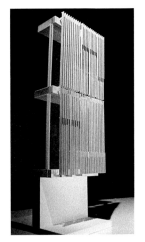

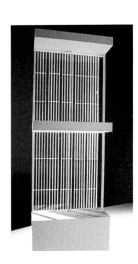

⅂ Mock-up showing louvers in different configurations.

∨ This diagram shows the louver shading concept. The slats adapt to climatic and programmatic needs to create optimal shading.

∧ This diagram shows the expanse of ceiling-mounted fans. Though the air is not cooled, the breeze created by the fans cool those in the immediate vicinity.

DINING HALL FANS CONCEPT

The concept for the Dining Hall was predicated on the idea that the space would be frequently open to the outside. To provide cooling without chilled air, swinging fans, an updated version of the traditional fans found in New Orleans before the advent of air conditioning, cool by means of circulating the air and creating a breeze. The fans are designed to be made from polycarbonate extrusions creating a luminous, lightweight structure that will reflect and animate light in the cafeteria.

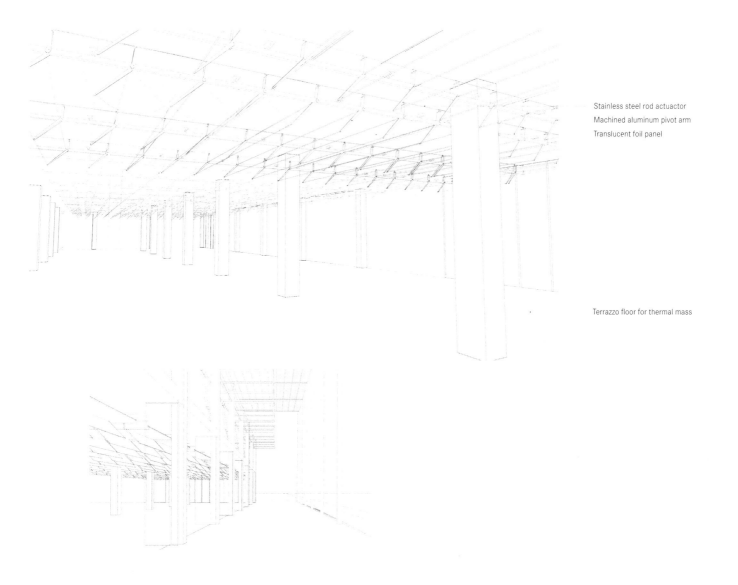

Stainless steel rod actuactor
Machined aluminum pivot arm
Translucent foil panel

Terrazzo floor for thermal mass

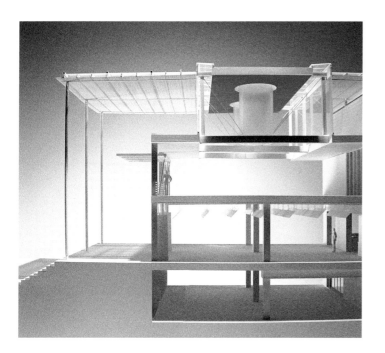

⌐^ Diagrams showing the expanse of ceiling mounted fans.

< Sectional model showing the cafeteria fans on the first floor and the ballroom fans on the second floor.

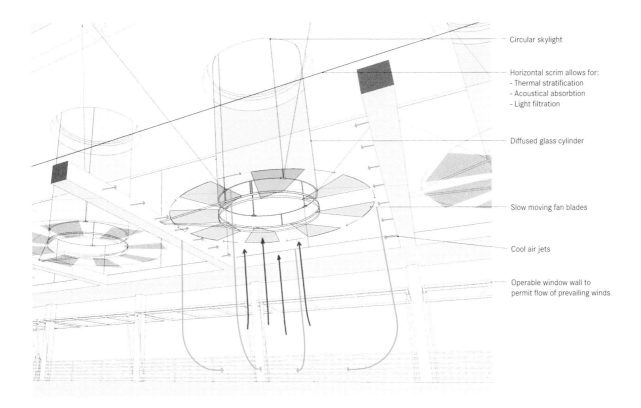

Circular skylight

Horizontal scrim allows for:
- Thermal stratification
- Acoustical absorbtion
- Light filtration

Diffused glass cylinder

Slow moving fan blades

Cool air jets

Operable window wall to
permit flow of prevailing winds

^ This diagram illustrates the cooling operation: cool air, emerging from ducts, travels down through the space, becomes warmer and is drawn up through the glass tubes.

< Model view of the ballroom fan concept: diffused glass is integrated into the design to provide light, transforming the typical HVAC system into an integral part of the architecture.

BALLROOM FANS CONCEPT

The concept for the ballroom ventilation makes use of its location on the second floor. Cool air jets are supplied from ducts into the downward stream of air created by the slow moving fan blades. Once the cool air absorbs more heat and rises upwards, it is evacuated through the diffused glass cylinders whose sun-heated skylight-tops create an updraft. The top of the glass tubes are planes of fritted glass with vents to the side, creating a hot surface that produces the convection effect that pulls warm air out of the space. The air escapes through vents at the cylinders' circumference. The breeze of the fans helps to cool the skin, while the low-emissivity coated horizontal scrim overhead helps isolate the cooler zone, removing the need to cool the whole space. The design allows for natural ventilation: during the temperate months, the ballroom is open fully to the outside.

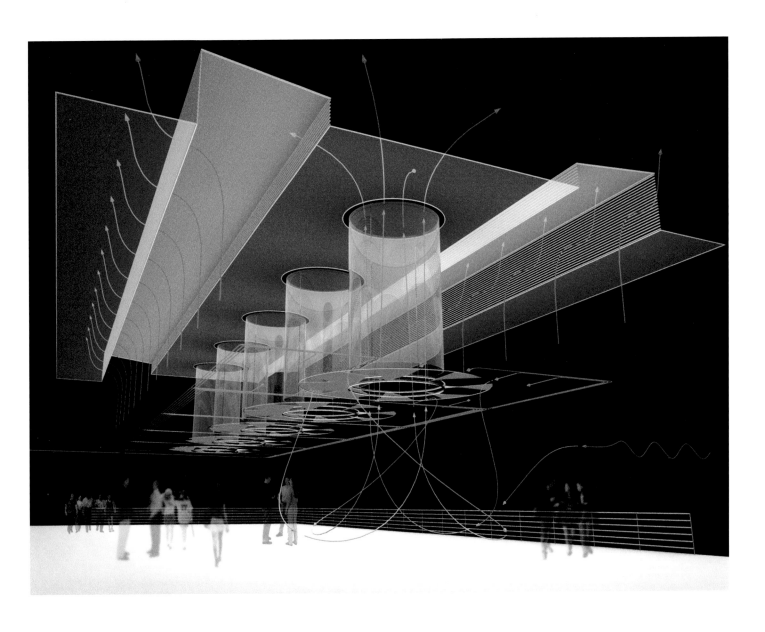

∧ This diagram illustrates the movement of air as it is cooled, becomes warmer and is extracted through the glass cylinders and through the scrim that also helps segregate temperature zones, absorb noise, and filter light.

↖ Full-scale mock-up of waterwall shown during testing.

↗↗ Diagram showing the movement of air and temperature exchange.

WATERWALL CONCEPT

The design of the waterwalls provides a dramatic environment for its intended purpose as an entrance zone, bridging together the inside of the building and the Commons and park outside. The two waterwalls are each 23 foot (7m) high and consist of chilled water running down a fine stainless steel mesh to create a translucent and activated surface. The concept for the waterwalls is similar to that of the ballroom fans but uses chilled water. The water comes from the central chiller plant, which turns the waterwalls into a giant dehumidifier: as cool water travels down the wall, the pendulum fans force the warmer humid air to condense into the waterfall and exchange heat with it, cooling the air and providing a breeze. As the air heats it rises and escapes through the ceiling scrim.

Perimeter skylight allows for:
- Daylight to interact with motion of fans
- Illumination of the water wall

Horizontal scrim allows for:
- Thermal stratification
- Acoustical absorption
- Light filtration

Gently oscillating
pendulum fans

Chilled water wall for
dehumidification and cooling

⌐ Model showing the connection between the building commons and the garden.

v This diagram illustrates the movement of air as it circulates, is cooled and dehumidified, warms and dissipates through the thermal scrim. The range of temperature is represented from warm to cool as red, yellow, green, and blue.

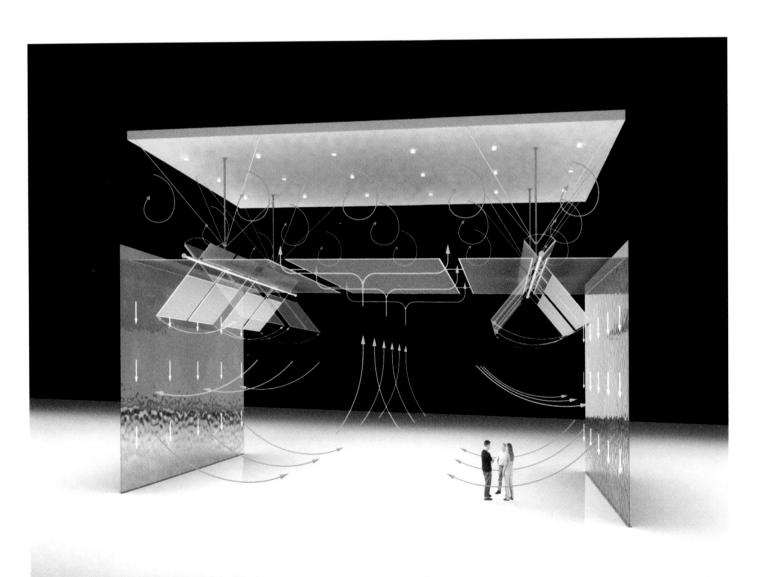

LUMINOUS THRESHOLD

^ Photograph of pedestrians crossing the Luminous Threshold.

The Luminous Threshold was designed as a gateway to the Olympic Complex in Sydney, Australia for the 2000 Summer Olympic Games. The complex, situated about 14km (8.7 miles) west of the city center, is a 760 hectare (2.9 square miles) waterfront site in the demographic heart of Sydney and includes major areas of environmental significance such as tidal mangrove swamps, a eucalyptus forest, and a casurarina woodland. Since the primary emphasis for the Olympics was the reclamation and recycling of a post-industrial landscape, all construction and artworks were sensitive to or expository of this relationship with the land.

The Luminous Threshold draws its inspiration from this mandate. The work is a threshold of light that perpendicularly crosses the northern entry to the park, sited parallel to an existing stream flowing through a mangrove-lined embankment. The design uses a sequence of five 23m (75 foot) high misting masts, at the top of which a singular and ever changing display of light can be seen as one approaches and leaves the park. By focusing on the ordering and changing nature of light as it intersects the mist, the Luminous Threshold creates an ephemeral landmark that celebrates the landscape and the 2000 Olympics in the sky overhead.

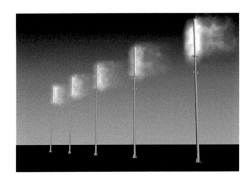

^^ Observations of light conditions common in the city were an early inspiration for the Luminous Threshold.

^ Rendering demonstrating the project's concept.

^ Mock-up of the misting system at top of masts.

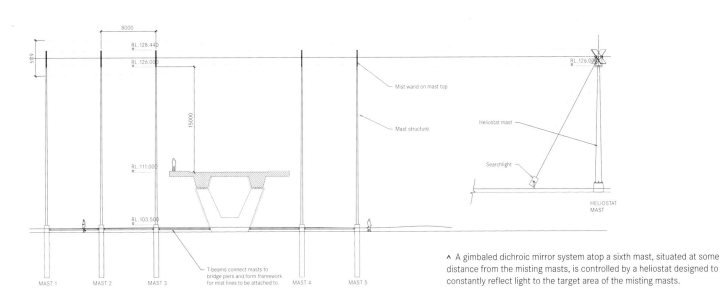

^ A gimbaled dichroic mirror system atop a sixth mast, situated at some distance from the misting masts, is controlled by a heliostat designed to constantly reflect light to the target area of the misting masts.

∧> Photographs of the exploration for the project, views of the installation, a detail of the misting device, and an aerial view of the Luminous Threshold in its context.

Observing urban light in humid and misty conditions, JCDA's team saw the opportunity to embody light through the medium of atmospheric water. By exploring existing misting technology and experimenting with various mirrors and coatings, JCDA established the feasibility of directing light through mist.

At the top of each mast is a 2.4m (8 foot) high stainless steel assembly with a series of nozzles that disperse a fine cloud of mist into the air. The drifting cloud of mist is animated by reflecting a yellow/gold stream of sunlight through its center and off of a system of mirrors. Controlled by a Heliostat and programmed to follow the sun's path throughout the day, the mirror system, comprised of a 10 x 10 foot (3 x 3m) set of nine dichroic-coated glass elements, consistently reflects a yellow/gold hue of light through the misters. This "dichroic" effect is achieved by applying layers of transparent metal deposits to the glass elements; the intensity and hue of the color is then determined by the sequencing of these layers.

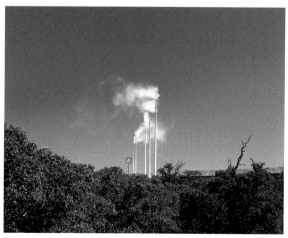

SOLAR REFLECTOR SHELL

New York | New York | 2004

^ Model showing interior shell with metal-faceted daylight lining.

Through a competition to integrate art into the design of the Fulton Street Center, James Carpenter Design Associates went a step further by collaborating with architects, Grimshaw & Partners, New York, to articulate light throughout their design. The master plan for the MTA Downtown Transit Center calls for the new Fulton Subway Station to be linked to the new World Trade Center Path Station by a cross-town subterranean pedestrian passageway. Significantly, the Fulton Street Transit Center establishes a new identity for the transit system in which light and daylight are a signatory element.

Carpenter's team proposed a metal lining that would float off the surface of the dome above the station. The team devised a perforated metal panel system inside the dome on its northern side to reflect light into the tunnels below and to capture and animate the passage of the sun projected through the dome's oculus, thereby fulfilling the architect's emphasis on the vertical connection between the street level and the subterranean pedestrian tunnels.

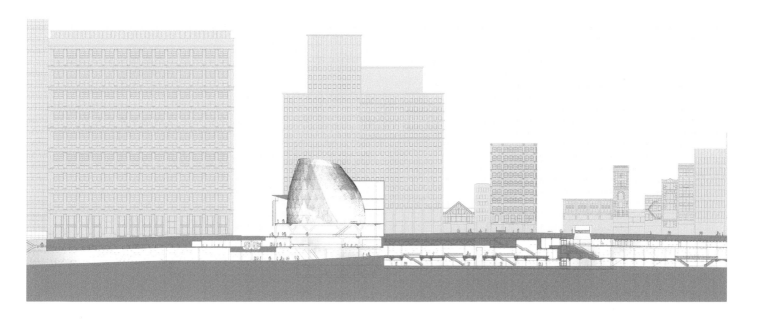

^ Cross section of Fulton Street Transit Center showing dome and connecting underground tunnels.

> Model of dome design with metal lining, bringing light down below ground onto the tracks.

∨ Section showing the entrance design and transition into the subway tunnels and tracks.

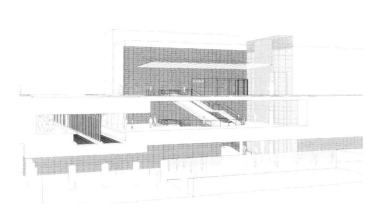

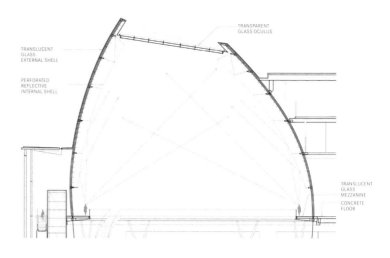

TRANSPARENT
GLASS OCULUS

TRANSLUCENT
GLASS
EXTERNAL SHELL

PERFORATED
REFLECTIVE
INTERNAL SHELL

TRANSLUCENT
GLASS
MEZZANINE

CONCRETE
FLOOR

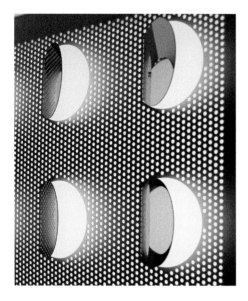

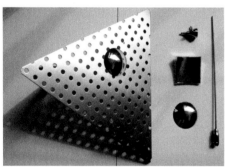

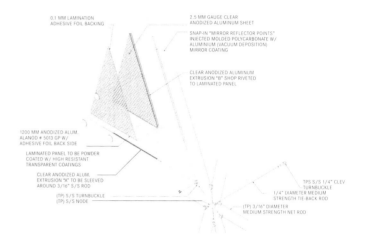

0.1 MM LAMINATION
ADHESIVE FOIL BACKING

2.5 MM GAUGE CLEAR
ANODIZED ALUMINUM SHEET

SNAP-IN "MIRROR REFLECTOR POINTS"
INJECTED MOLDED POLYCARBONATE W/
ALUMINIUM (VACUUM DEPOSITION)
MIRROR COATING

CLEAR ANODIZED ALUMINUM
EXTRUSION "B" SHOP RIVETED
TO LAMINATED PANEL

1200 MM ANODIZED ALUM.
ALANOD # 5013 GP W/
ADHESIVE FOIL BACK SIDE

LAMINATED PANEL TO BE POWDER
COATED W/ HIGH RESISTANT
TRANSPARENT COATINGS

CLEAR ANODIZED ALUM.
EXTRUSION "A" TO BE SLEEVED
AROUND 3/16" S/S ROD

(TP) S/S TURNBUCKLE
(TP) S/S NODE

TPS S/S 1/4" CLEV
TURNBUCKLE
1/4" DIAMETER MEDIUM
STRENGTH TIE-BACK ROD

(TP) 3/16" DIAMETER
MEDIUM STRENGTH NET ROD

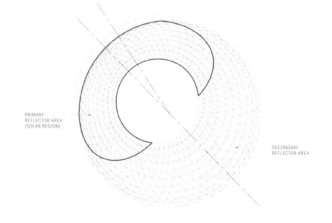

PRIMARY
REFLECTOR AREA
(SOLAR REGION)

SECONDARY
REFLECTOR AREA

^^ Early concept for reflective elements of the perforated metal panels.

^ Point reflector panel.

ᴎᴎ Section of dome identifying materials and viewing angles up into the dome.

ᴎ Detail drawing of connection of perforated panels.

>↙ Primary and secondary reflector area map of inner dome.

Established through a series of tests, the interior dome
surfaces combine diffused and mirrored metal in a pattern
that suggests the rotation of the earth. These fragments
of mirror project shafts of light down to the lowest depths
of the station. The geometry of the dome and its metal
lining was analyzed and refined to optimize the orientation
and reflection of daylight. At night, the dome is lit from
within through strategic interactive artificial lighting.

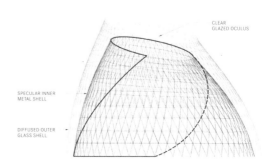

CLEAR
GLAZED OCULUS

SPECULAR INNER
METAL SHELL

DIFFUSED OUTER
GLASS SHELL

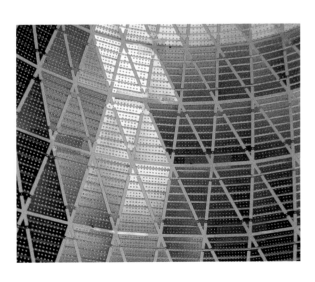

∧ Rendering of the dome showing the metal inner shell capturing the sun's path as it is projected through the dome's oculus.

< Acid-etched metal scale model of the inner shell.

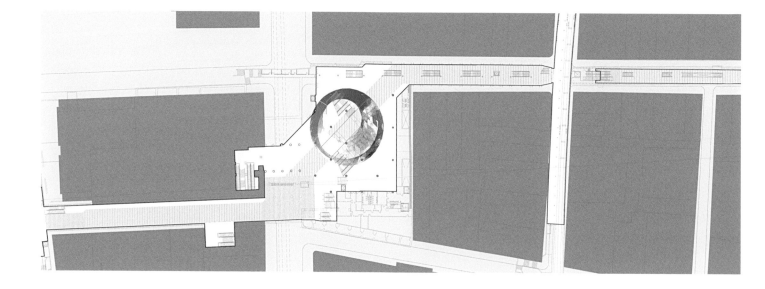

∧ Competition drawing showing the below ground pedestrian tunnels as they intersect the Fulton Street Transit Center.

∨ Computer simulations showing the variable interactive lighting levels.

JCDA proposed integrating the lighting scheme into the experience of the tunnels. The new Dey Street Tunnel and the revitalization of the Fulton Street Tunnels offered the opportunity to relieve the sense of compression experienced by pedestrians during times of overcrowding. By addressing the proportional configuration of the tunnels and by programming materials that can embody light, JCDA could produce a perceptual expansion of space. The play of light, reflection, and projection extends the walls and ceiling beyond their physical limits while the pedestrians shifting perspective activates the play of light.

JCDA's scheme to light the tunnels envisions one wall as the primary lighting source: a glowing surface that can be linked to video or motion sensors to create changes in the movement of light through the tunnel. This interactive wall is controlled by the movement of the pedestrians. The source of the illumination is behind a layer of slotted and perforated stainless steel. Light emerging through these slots reflects off the ceiling and opposite wall. The surfaces actively conduct and reflect light and images of pedestrian movement along the tunnel, thereby creating the perception of depth beyond the tunnel surfaces.

∧ Mock-up model used to test light effects.

∨ This early study model shows the intent of using punched stainless steel wall surfaces with suppressed lighting.

SPORTS FACILITY

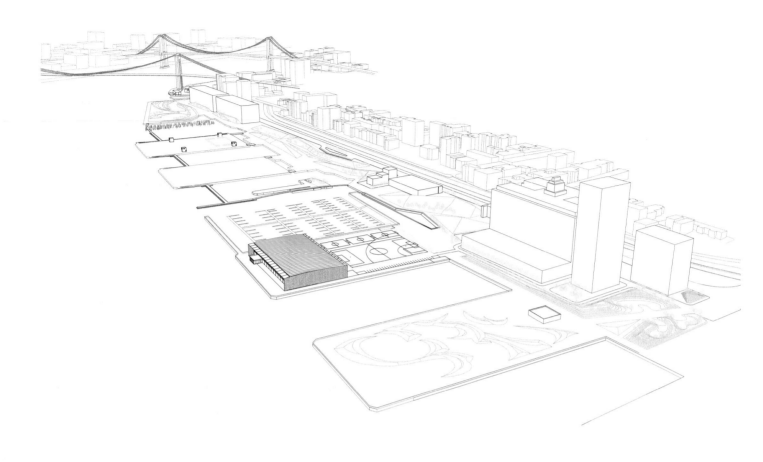

^ Aerial perspective of the lightweight sports enclosure in its park context.

↗ Renderings of the structure at dusk.

> Renderings of the Sports Facility, exterior and interior. As an extremely lightweight material, the EFTE roof allows for smaller trusses (spanning 200 foot with a 10 foot depth (61 m, 3 m) at the mid-span), maximizing interior clearance for the soccer field.

As part of the redevelopment of the Brooklyn waterfront, this site was designated to provide local high schools and the public with access to much needed year-round athletic facilities. JCDA was invited by the landscape architect, Michael Van Valkenburgh & Associates, to design an architectural and structural concept for Brooklyn Bridge Park's sports enclosure to be built at the end of the 400 x 800 foot (122 x 244m) Pier 5, on the Brooklyn Waterfront south of Brooklyn Bridge.

JCDA proposed a lightweight steel building with an enclosing skin designed to optimize solar conditions and prevailing winds while providing dramatic views to and from the harbor and Lower Manhattan. The multi-use recreation building accommodates a high school soccer field and can be used for a variety of community functions. The structure is semi-conditioned and naturally ventilated, acting as an open-air facility during the spring, summer and fall, and an "outdoor room" during the winter.

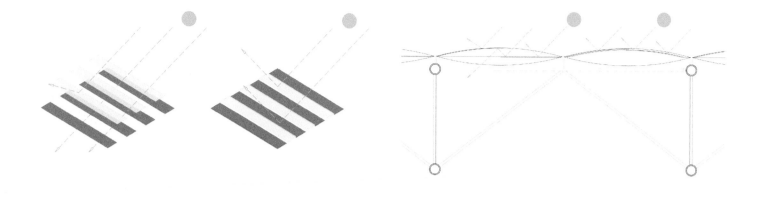

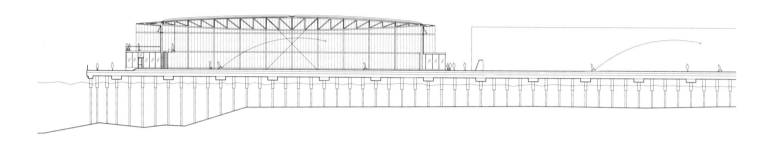

^^ Adjustment of EFTE foil patterns creates different heating and lighting conditions.

^ Section showing the Sports Facility on its site on the pier.

The simple 230 x 350 x 45 foot (70 x 107 x 14m) volume of the structure uses new material technology to capitalize on the site's unusual limitations. The result is a lightweight, low cost and intelligent building. The roof of the Sports Facility is comprised of linear inflated EFTE foil "pillows" (ethyltetrafluoroethylene, a fluoropolymer material). The pillows contain one clear and two printed, patterned layers of EFTE foil. The air pressure in the two air pockets is adjusted to create an open or closed pattern, thereby controlling heat radiation and lighting.

To optimize comfort, the roof pillows allow more solar energy to enter the building on sunny winter days; shut out the sun's direct rays on summer days; and provide insulation during the winter. Insulation and solar heat are bolstered by radiant heating and cooling located beneath the surface of the synthetic playing field. Instead of fuel, this system uses a heat exchange system set in the water below the pier to minimize heating and cooling costs.

For day-lighting, the roof's transparency can be adjusted to accommodate both overcast and sunny days. At night the roof system allows for changes in levels of luminosity both externally and internally. The west and east walls are highly transparent insulated glass units, and the north and south walls are planes of translucent polycarbonate insulation that glow with diffused light in the interior during the day and on the exterior at night. The polycarbonate end walls create even light behind the soccer goals and help to frame views through the clear west wall to the harbor and Lower Manhattan.

At night, the hall's luminosity makes it visible throughout the harbor, while during the day the rippled surface of the roof pillows merges with the shimmering surface of the river's reflected and transmitted light.

^ Large, operable glass doors open along the east and west walls, reinforcing the views from the park through the building to the harbor and city beyond while allowing the breeze from the water to cool the space during warmer months.

THE WORK OF JAMES CARPENTER DESIGN AND ASSOCIATES
by Kenneth Frampton

James Carpenter is a unique practitioner, but in what field exactly it is hard to say. He is an artist whose development was profoundly influenced by an intense involvement with an essential aspect of modern building technology—namely plate glass in all its multifarious applications. So, while he was first trained briefly in architecture and then in sculpture at the Rhode Island School of Design, graduating in 1972, the singularly most decisive experience of his formation as a designer seems to have been the decade that he subsequently spent as a consultant to the Corning Glass Works in Corning, New York. In this undertaking he was sponsored by Thomas Buechner, director of the Corning Museum of Glass, felt that it would be advantageous for the company to have a talent-ed in-house artist involved in the research and development. While Carpenter continued to work as an independent artist, the advisory position enabled him to participate in the evolution of new materials, including photo-responsive glass and various forms of vitreous ceramics. Most of the research in which he participated was oriented towards architecture as the field most capa-ble of utilizing sophisticated glass technology as a new means for manipulating light, shade, and surface effect.

Much of the Corning research focused on the development of interference coatings and on the pro-duction of different forms of dichroic glass. While restricted throughout his initial practice to the creation of various special features and glass membranes installed in buildings largely designed by others, Carpenter was obliged to devote much of his energies to the manner in which the glass was secured. This inevitably led him into the related field of metal fabrication in order to optimize the environmental and phenomenological potential of glass. This entry into the structural use of mutu-ally interacting materials, with different coefficients of expansion, prompted him, after his experi-ence at Corning, to seek out specialists and collaborators of exceptional caliber, both within his own studio and without, in particular structural and environmental engineers. The widening scope of Carpenter's practice also entailed the cultivation of specialist fabricators that he knew would be able to supply the quality production he was after; most notably, in the late 1980s, ship's chan-dlers such as Navtec of Westford, MA, which later became TriPyramid Structures, Inc. The need to maintain precision at every level from fabrication to installation encouraged Carpenter to cultivate a staff whose design prowess was matched by their ability to supervise and, even further, to develop a capacity for the erection of the works on site.

By the early 1990s, Carpenter's practice began to gain a certain renown outside the U.S., above all in Germany, where he was asked to collaborate with Günter Behnisch & Partner on the design of a tensile dome sculpture for the Bonn Parliament, built in 1991. Designed in association with

Richard Kress and Luke Lowings, both of whom had by then become core members of his studio team, this work, neither architecture nor sculpture in the conventional sense, led what is now the firm of James Carpenter Design Associates (JCDA) into the field of tensile net construction. They would later continue in this genre, experimenting with wire-cable suspension structures ranging from a tensile net stair designed for a home in Chicago in 1993 to an inverted wire-cable and translucent glass dome in the Richard Meier & Partners' Sandra Day O'Connor Court-house in 1998.

Carpenter's first collaboration with the German engineer Jörg Schlaich came in 1991, when they worked together on a project for a twin-mast, cable-stayed bridge over the Mississippi River in St. Paul, Minnesota. In 1996, when the architects Müller Reimann invited Carpenter and Schlaich to collaborate on their competition entry for the German Foreign Ministry in Berlin, the two jointly developed and detailed the glazed atrium, or Lichthof. As with the subsequent glazed façade of the Time Warner Building, New York, the 150 foot (46 m) high glazed, cable-net entry façade of the Berlin ministry was sustained by two sets of tensile cables separated from each other, one running vertically from floor to ceiling and the other horizontally from side to side. The stainless steel strut components that maintained the stability of this glass wall were extended to 17 inch (43 cm) long, cantilevering off the vertical wire cables and, at every course, clamped to the horizontal wire cables that sustain the internal membrane. This separates the structure from the glass and creates a reflected sense of depth to the threshold.

With this work the Carpenter office would pass from the limited scope of sensitively detailed, inge-nious building elements to the more comprehensive task of creating a total microclimate. In the Lichthof project JCDA was involved not only with the cable-net wall but also with the design of the vaulted glass roofs covering the court, each vault supported on lenticular trusses. These roof vaults were fitted with translucent anti-solar glass so as to admit narrow shafts of sunlight at certain times of the day. At the same time, metal reflector panels applied to the structural girders that support the vaults reflect daylight back into the darkest part of the courtyard. In fact, the entire roof functions in phenomenological terms as a sky reflector, projecting the sun and sky back onto the inner surface of the cable-net glass wall facing north. A band of clear glass frames the expanse of semi-reflective glass, permitting one to sense the layering of views and reflections seen through and on the cable-net wall.

To date, the largest membrane to be realized to the designs of JCDA is the 50 story reconstructed 7 World Trade Center, New York. Here the overall frame, structure, and internal organization were the responsibility of the corporate architects Skidmore, Owings & Merrill, under the direction of David Childs, while the overall appearance of the finished structure was developed by the Carpenter studio in close collaboration with Skidmore, Owings & Merrill. In this instance, the most difficult challenge was to devise two different membrane systems that would each be appropriate to the volumes they contained: Con-Edison transformers in eight stories of concrete and a 42 story office building. To this end, both membranes were designed to be equally responsive to the changing incidence and intensity of the natural light. JCDA faced the concrete transformer station with a continuous grill comprised of two layers of vertical stainless steel prismatic wires of varying triangular section and setting, while for the bulk of the office tower the team designed a double-glazed curtain wall, comprising a glass membrane, linear-lapped and set above recessed and curved spandrel panels at each floor. The inner surface of these panels are corrugated and embossed so as to serve as sky reflectors, and this blue stainless steel sill picks up the local light conditions causing the curtain wall to merge with the color of the sky. The low-iron glass used yields a highly transparent membrane, while the corner columns were inset so as to heighten the illusion of dematerializing mass. Thus, aside from the normal glistening effect that one associates with curtain wall construction, the crystalline shaft of the tower appears to emanate light at every floor.

One of the most remarkable aspects of this work is the stainless steel revetment enveloping the eight story concrete podium. The double layered grillwork, in relief, is visually activated day and night in two different but related ways. During the day, a dynamic optical effect is obtained partly through the varying incidence of the natural light as it strikes the prismatic grillwork and partly through a constantly transposing iteration of highlights arising directly out of the movement of the observer. During the night, the rear layer of the grillwork is animated by blue and white light projected from LEDs mounted on the back of the front grillwork. As twilight descends, this blue luminosity within the stainless steel matrix assumes the image of a cubic volume that by corresponding to the upper space of the foyer serves perceptually to anchor the core of the tower shaft into the stainless steel base.

In the foyer itself, a 65 foot long, 14 foot high (19.8 x 4.3m) translucent glass wall behind the reception desk serves to display a scrolling, commemorative inscription designed by the artist Jenny Holzer and JCDA. Due to the use of diffusion glass, Holzer's LED memorial message passes across this monumental illusory plane like a mirage, taking on different levels of legibility depending upon the viewer's position. Here we are returned to Marshall McLuhan's "the medium is the message." The ineffability of light is ultimately the common medium upon which the work of both Holzer and

Carpenter is equally dependent. Neither quite belongs, as it were, to the artistic field in which they might be said to have their origins. Both gravitate toward an expanded field: Holzer towards literature if not poetry in the original sense of *poesis* and Carpenter towards architecture, in the sense of *architecton* – chief constructor. It may be argued that because of its literary and somewhat cryptically representational character, Holzer's work is neither a mural nor a sculpture; just as in this instance, Carpenter's illusory luminous environment is neither quite architecture nor art.

Four projects designed in the last ten years make us progressively aware of the way in which, without relinquishing his focus on the membrane, Carpenter has moved towards the broader scope of the total micro-environment.

The first and most metaphoric work in this sequence is the "Luminous Threshold" projected in 1998 for the 2000 Sydney Olympics. A typical Carpenter work in that the phenomenological effects arise out of a dynamic interplay between nature and culture. In this instance, the filtered and focused rays of the sun and micro-cloud formations issue from a series of jets mounted on top of the masts. He speaks of this work as emulating the phenomena of "sun halos." In point of fact both manifestations depend on a subtle manipulation of technology, whereby the interplay of natural phenomena comes to be revealed through artificial means. This minimalist environmental work, at a civic scale, embodies a postmodernist sculptural dimension by virtue of being neither exactly landscape nor architecture. In this regard it bears comparison to Walter de Maria's Lightning Field erected in the wilds of New Mexico in 1977.

Carpenter enters more fully into the environmental mode in his work with the Minnesota architect Vincent James; together they designed the new student center in Tulane University, a project dating from 1999. In collaboration with the German environmental engineer Matthias Schuler of Transsolar Engineering, JCDA envisioned a "verandah" building for this renovation and expansion of an existing student center, planned on three floors, around a pre-existing core, with the last reorganized to accommodate two medium-sized lecture halls and a refectory. The basic sustainable precept complementing this verandah concept is the use of passive cooling and ventilation as progressive climatic boundaries around the perimeter of the building. The salient strategy was to treat most of the ground floor as a "tempered zone," while utilizing centralized air-conditioning for the lower ground floor and a large part of the first floor. In this way, the perimeter of the ground floor could be handled as a partially conditioned microclimate, particularly on the southeast façade. A similar approach was taken towards the first floor ballroom situated to the north of the central core. The overall environmental strategy was to maintain a flexible permeability between the inside and outside of the structure, and to this end, Carpenter, together with James and Schuler, created a highly transformable design in which the ground floor common room may be fully opened up, either through sliding-folding glass walls or through vertically sliding plate glass window walls, 9 foot (2.7m) in height. This last, under certain climatic conditions, will be slid up as counterbalanced sash windows behind the fixed upper half of the window wall. Such an innovative glazing provision is matched by the equally large vertically pivoting windows that are to be used to ventilate the ballroom on the first floor. Deep lightweight canopies in perforated metal constitute the actual verandah and shield the southwestern and northeastern faces of the building, while aluminum-reinforced operable wood louvers are deployed as adjustable sun screens on the southeastern face. Ceiling fans of both the pendulum and rotary variety are to be widely deployed throughout, the cooling capacity of the latter greatly enhanced by blowing cold jets of air onto the blades of the fan.

It would be difficult to find any other medium-sized contemporary structure in North America, or even elsewhere, so well designed and equipped for the immediate modification of its varying microclimates through adjustable fenestration and ventilation. Close in its light modular character to Norman Foster's Carré d'Art media-tech completed in Nîmes in 1993, the Tulane Student center is also a work that recalls the highly ingenious, poetic, mechanical elaborations of Pierre Chareau's Maison de Verre of 1932. Like the domestic works of the Australian architect Glenn Murcutt, this is a building in which the membrane will require constant adjustment on the part of its user in order to maximize its potential.

With their joint 2004 proposal for the dome and tunnels of the MTA Fulton Street Transit Center, JCDA and Grimshaw & Partners have categorically demonstrated the possibility of providing a civilized environment for a subterranean east/west pedestrian interchange between the various transit lines running north/south in Manhattan. For the proposed 2,200 foot (670m) long tunnel system linking the various lines, 50% of which is already below ground, JCDA developed a stainless steel lining for the walls and the roof of the tunnel system and a partially reflective, partially translucent dome, open at the top, to be set above a multi-level concourse situated at the virtual midpoint of the transverse subterranean network. This conical reflector comprises an outer weatherproof glass skin with a partially perforated, reflective metal lining. Its outer form constitutes a monumental luminous feature rising well above the level of the surrounding streets. In addition to the aforementioned perforations designed to admit both natural and artificial light, there are reflective bosses implanted at intervals so as to disperse the sun's rays in a more focused way as they strike the inner surface of the dome. One is reminded of László Moholy-Nagy's Light Modulator of 1936, only now it is the sun that moves while the perforated surfaces are fixed. As with the perforated metal lining of the tunnels, where an LED system behind the screen walls and ceiling is constantly activated by the passage of the pedestrians through the tunnels, Carpenter's dome is equipped with artificial lighting between the clear glass exterior skin and the diffused glass-cum-reflective surface of the inner membrane; thus its luminosity may be modulated day and night throughout the seasons.

Up to now Carpenter's penchant for lightweight minimalist structure has never been more economically demonstrated than in his proposal for erecting a 180 by 300 foot, 45 foot high (55 x 91 x 14 m) shed to accommodate an indoor soccer field and multipurpose space on the top of a disused pier as a part of Michael Van Valkenburgh's masterplan for the Brooklyn Bridge Riverfront Park. This dematerialized shed will be equipped with sliding glass doors on its eastern and western elevations so that on temperate days a large part of the 300 foot (91 m) membrane may be opened out so as to not only facilitate ventilation but also to afford totally unobstructed views of the water from the park. Still in process, the initial structural concept comprised 180 foot (55 m) span self-bracing triangulated support system that will transmit the structural load via hinged joints to the concrete grade beams and timber pile structure that makes up the fabric of the existing pier. The roof, a translucent ETFE air cushion roof, is a new form of plastic covering (ethyl tetra fluoro ethylene) consisting of a triple layered, translucent, self-insulating film, a tenth of the weight of glass. The upper two layers are printed in a counter pattern so that when the lower layer of the triple skin fabric is inflated with air the two fretted surfaces are overlaid in such a manner as to obscure most of the sun. Controlled by servo-mechanisms, this air may be heated in the winter to melt the snow. Conversely, when the upper layer is under a marginally higher pressure the layers are separated so as to admit sunlight.

Carpenter envisages integrating photovoltaic cells into the uppermost fretted layer of the fabric to offset the amount of electricity consumed by the structure. The overall sustainability of the building also depends on cooling the space with a heat pump-chiller fed directly by the water of the river, alternatively heating and cooling, with the cool air delivered to the volume through a radiant pipe system below the playing field. From Brooklyn Heights, Carpenter imagines the whole structure hovering like a luminous lantern above the water at night, while during the day, the glistening, undulating surface of the roof will establish a visually empathetic relationship with the rippling sheen of the river.

By now the scope of JCDA's activities is so expanded as to defy classification, particularly since Carpenter's self-conscious cultivation of collaborative design has now become so well-orchestrated, dynamic, and transnational as to resemble the concerted effort of a highly advanced, research laboratory rather than an artist's or architect's studio in the conventional sense. This condition finds confirmation in Carpenter's meticulous habit of directly crediting virtually every significant member of the design team assembled for each project, so that the attribution more closely resembles the credit line at the end of a feature film than that which is normally provided by our anachronistic mythical misconceptions about individual creativity, even though leadership and inventive ingenuity are obviously always present throughout the process. Like film, environmental design at any consequential scale is a collective endeavor, and it always has been so, no matter who may be ultimately directing and guiding the final outcome. Carpenter's luminous environmentalism lies closer—in more ways than one—to the sublime "almost nothing" of the German Enlightenment, to the *beinahe nichts,* as Mies van der Rohe was fond of saying.

Neither sculpture nor landscape, although it shares with the latter a preoccupation with the nature/culture interface, Carpenter's work gravitates towards architecture, while simultaneously veering away from it. Although it remains against representation, even in the case of the somewhat emblematic misting masts that he designed for Sydney, it is invariably focused on the generation of an intensely membranous aesthetic which, while discreetly acknowledging the lost cause of the ornamental, attempts to transcend this loss. It is a practice that compels us to relinquish any received taxonomy of the arts. Evading the cynical reactionary aspects of postmodernism through a culture of technology, Carpenter remains, rather than any other category that we might be tempted to ascribe to his production, like August Perret and Jean Prouvé before him, *un constructeur par excellance*.

CONFINES
Filmed in 1975
Shown in 1978 at the John Gibson Gallery, New York, New York
Super-eight film loop
Conception, installation, production: James Carpenter
Camera work, installation: Dan Reiser, Tom Payne

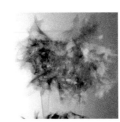

SHAKING
Filmed in 1978
Super-eight film loop
Conception, installation, production: James Carpenter
Camera work, installation: Dan Reiser

CAUSE
Filmed in 1975–1976
Shown in 1978 at the John Gibson Gallery, New York, New York
Super-eight film loop
Conception, installation, production: James Carpenter
Camera work, installation: Dan Reiser, Tom Payne

ORIENTATION
Filmed in 1978
Shown in 1979 at the John Gibson Gallery, New York, New York
Super-eight film loop
Conception, installation, production: James Carpenter
Camera work, installation, production: Dan Reiser, Tom Payne, Dan Trupiano

TAILS OF FATE
Filmed in 1975
Super-eight film loop
Conception, installation, production: James Carpenter

WOLF PACK
Filmed in 1979
Super-eight film loops
Conception, installation, production: James Carpenter

TRACKS
Filmed in 1977
Super-eight film loops
Conception, installation, production: James Carpenter

WHIRLPOOL
Filmed in 1980
Super-eight film loops
Conception, installation, production: James Carpenter

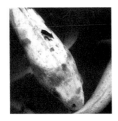

KOI
Filmed in 1979–1980
Super-eight film loops
Conception, installation, production: James Carpenter
Camera work, installation: Dan Reiser

HOMING
Filmed in 1978
Shown in 1978 at the Clocktower Gallery, New York, New York and in 1980 at the John Gibson Gallery, New York, New York
Super-eight film loop
Conception, installation, production: James Carpenter
Camera work, installation: Dan Reiser

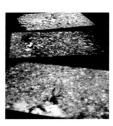

MIGRATION
Filmed in 1978
Shown in 1978 at the John Gibson Gallery, New York, New York and at Galerie Nächst St. Stephan, Vienna, Austria
Super-eight film loops
Conception, installation, production: James Carpenter
Camera work: Buster Simpson
Installation: Dan Reiser

STRUCTURAL GLASS PRISMS 1985–1987
Indianapolis, Indiana
Client: Christian Theological Seminary, Indianapolis
Architect: Edward Larrabee Barnes
Design principal: James Carpenter
Project team: Dan Reiser, Vera Marjanovic

LUMINOUS GLASS BRIDGE 1987
Marin County, California
Client: Private
Structural engineer: Ove Arup & Partners
Design principal: James Carpenter
Project team: Michael Morris, Yoshiko Sato

GLASS TRUSS ROD WALL 1988–1991
Los Angeles, California
Architect: Skidmore Owings & Merrill
Engineer: Ove Arup, Tony Broomhead
Design principal: James Carpenter
Project team: Neil Logan, Luke Lowings, Janet Fink, Richard Kress

OREGON HEALTH SCIENCES UNIVERSITY GLASS FLOOR 1989–1991
Portland, Oregon
Architect: Richard Meier and Partners
Design principal: James Carpenter
Project team: Neil Logan, Luke Lowings, Janet Fink, Richard Kress
Installation: Brian Gulick

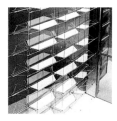

ARCH TRUSS WALL 1988–1989
Los Angeles, California
Architect: Johnson, Fain & Pereira
Engineer: Ove Arup & Partners, Tony Broomhead
Design principal: James Carpenter
Senior designer: Janet Fink
Project team: Neil Logan, Richard Kress, Luke Lowings

TENSION NET SCULPTURE 1990
Los Angeles, California
Client: Southern California Gas Company, Los Angeles
Design principal: James Carpenter
Senior designer: Richard Kress
Project team: Janet Fink, Luke Lowings, Neil Logan

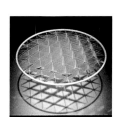

CHILDREN'S CHAPEL WINDOW 1990
Manhasset, New York
Client: Unitarian Universalist Church, Manhasset
Architect: Edward Larrabee Barnes
Design principal: James Carpenter
Senior designer: Richard Kress
Installation: Brian Gulick, Greg Morrell
Glass: Depp Glass
Fittings: Tripyramid Structures

TENSION DOME ROOF 1990
Bonn, Germany
Client: Bonn Parliament, Bonn
Architect: Behnisch & Partner
Design principal: James Carpenter
Senior designer: Richard Kress

SHELL OCULUS PROPOSAL 1990
Genoa, Italy
Client: Genoa Aquarium, Genoa
Architect: Renzo Piano Building Workshop, Cambridge Seven Associates
Design principal: James Carpenter
Senior designer: Richard Kress
Project team: Luke Lowings

REFRACTIVE TENSEGRITY RINGS 1991
Munich, Germany
Client: BMW Munich Airport, Munich, Germany
Engineer: Ove Arup & Partners, Tony Broomhead
Design principal: James Carpenter
Senior designer: Luke Lowings
Installation: Brian Gulick, Greg Morrell, Richard Kress
Glass: Depp Glass
Fittings: Tripyramid Structures

TWIN MAST BRIDGE PROPOSAL 1992–1994
St. Paul, Minnesota
Client: City of St. Paul, Wabasha Street Bridge Commission, St. Paul
Engineer: Schlaich Bergermann und Partner, Jörg Schlaich, Hans Schober, TKDA & Associates
Design principal: James Carpenter
Senior designer: Luke Lowings
Project team: Janet Fink, Richard Kress

REFRACTIVE GLASS WALL 1992
City Honolulu, Hawaii
Client: First Hawaiian Bank
Architect: Kohn Pedersen Fox
Glazing consult: Rayme Kuniyuki, Heintges Architects
Consultants
Design principal: James Carpenter
Senior designer: Ali Tayar
Project team: Rebecca Uss
Glass: Depp Glass
Fittings: Tripyramid Structures

LIGHT PORTAL 1995–2006
Center Artery Tunnel, Boston, Massachusetts
Client: Central Artery Tunnel, Authority, Boston
Architect and structural engineer: Bechtel/Parsons
Brinkerhoff
Design principal: James Carpenter
Senior designer: Luke Lowings
Project team: Richard Kress, Rebecca Uss, Marek
Walczak, Katherine Wyberg, Aki Ishida
Installation: Brian Gulick

RETRACTING SCREEN 1993
Dallas, Texas
Client: Howard Rachofsky
Architect: Richard Meier & Partners
Fabrication: Canstruct, Tripyramid Structures
Glass manufacturer: Depp Glass
Design principal: James Carpenter
Senior designer: Luke Lowings
Installation: Brian Gulick, Greg Morrell

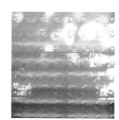

PERISCOPE WINDOW 1995–1997
Minneapolis, Minnesota
Client: Private
Architect: Vincent James Associates, Architects
Design principal: James Carpenter
Senior designer: Marek Walzcak
Project team: Rebecca Uss, Richard Kress
Installation: Brian Gulick
Structure: Product + Design
Glass: Depp Glass

TENSION NET STAIR 1993–1995
Chicago, Illinois
Client: Private
Architect: Larson Associates
Engineer: Dewhurst Macfarlane
Design principal: James Carpenter
Senior designer: Luke Lowings
Installation: Brian Gulick, Greg Morrell, Mark McClellan
Glass: Depp Glass
Fittings: Tripyramid Structures

LUMINOUS GATEWAY PROPOSAL 1996
Stamford, Connecticut
Client: Swiss Bank
Architect: Skidmore, Owings & Merrill
Design principal: James Carpenter
Project team: Richard Kress, Marek Walczak

SCULPTURAL LIGHT REFLECTORS 1994–2000
San Francisco, California
Client: San Francisco Arts Commission, San Francisco
International Airport, San Francisco
Architect: Skidmore, Owings & Merrill, Craig Hartman
Engineer: Buro Happold
Design principal: James Carpenter
Senior designer: Janet Fink
Project team: Richard Kress, Luke Lowings, Erik Schultz,
Rebecca Uss, Marek Walczak
Installation: Brian Gulick, Birdair

LENS CEILING 1996–2000
Sandra Day O'Connor Courthouse, Phoenix, Arizona
Client: General Services Administration
Architect: Richard Meier & Partners
Engineer: Ove Arup & Partners, Matt King
Components: TriPyramid Structures
Lighting designer: Fischer Marantz Renfro Stone
Design principal: James Carpenter
Senior designer: Luke Lowings
Project team: Richard Kress, Rebecca Uss, Marek
Walczak, Katherine Wyberg, Aki Ishida
Installation: Brian Gulick
Glass: Depp Glass

DICHROIC LIGHT FIELD 1994–1995
Columbus Avenue, New York, New York
Client: Millennium Partnership
Architect: Handel & Associates
Structural engineer: Desimone Chaplin & Dobrin
Design principal: James Carpenter
Senior designer: Luke Lowings
Project team: Janet Fink, Richard Kress
Glass: Depp Glass

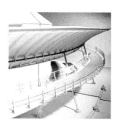

BREMERHAVEN RING BRIDGE PROPOSAL 1994
Bremerhaven, Germany
Client: City of Bremerhaven
Architect: Cambridge Seven Associates
Engineer: Schlaich Bergermann und Partner
Design principal: James Carpenter
Project team: Luke Lowings, Richard Kress, Rebecca Uss

SCOTTSDALE MUSEUM 1996
Scottsdale, Arizona
Architect: William Bruder Architects
Engineer: Rudow + Berry Structural Engineering
Design principal: James Carpenter
Project team: Aki Ishida, Rebecca Uss
Installation: Brian Gulick, Greg Morell
Glass: Depp Glass

SUSPENDED GLASS TOWER 1997
Convention and Exhibition Center Hong Kong
Client: Hong Kong Trade Development Council,
Hong Kong
Architect: Skidmore, Owings & Merrill
Engineer: Ove Arup & Partners, Tony Broomhead
Components: TriPyramid Structures Inc.
Design principal: James Carpenter
Senior designer: Richard Kress
Project team: Luke Lowings, Rebecca Uss, Janet Fink
Installation: Brian Gulick
Glass: Depp Glass

LICHTHOF 1997–1999
Berlin, Germany
Client: Federal Office for Construction and Regional
Planning, Germany
Architect: Müller Reimann Architekten
Engineer: Schlaich Bergermann und Partner, Stuttgart,
Jörg Schlaich, Hans Schober, Thomas Fackler
Design principal: James Carpenter
Senior designer: Luke Lowings
Project team: Richard Kress, Stephanie Forsythe

TENSION DOME 1997–1999
Charlotte, North Carolina
Client: Nations Bank, Charlotte
Engineer: David L. Kufferman, P.E.
Design principal: James Carpenter
Senior designer: Katherine Wyberg
Installation: Brian Gulick, Greg Morrell
Glass: Depp Glass
Fittings: Tripyramid Structures

RITZ CARLTON MILLENIA PROPOSAL 1997
Singapore
Design principal: James Carpenter
Senior designer: Richard Kress

LUMINOUS SUSPENDED BLUE ROOM
PROPOSAL 1997
Kurfürstendamm, Berlin, Germany
Client: DIFA Berlin
Architect: Murphy Jahn
Engineer: Werner Sobek
Design principal: James Carpenter
Senior designer: Richard Kress
Project team: Luke Lowings, Mary Springer

GREAT HALL LIGHT TOWER 1998
San Francisco Civic Center, San Francisco, California
Client: San Francisco Civic Center Complex Arts Program,
San Francisco
Architect: Skidmore, Owings & Merrill, Craig Hartman
Engineer: Ove Arup & Partners, Tony Broomhead
Design principal: James Carpenter
Senior designer: Richard Kress
Project team: Luke Lowings, Marek Walczak
Installation: Brian Gulick
Fittings: Tripyramid Structures

LIGHT MAST 1998–1999
Cincinnati, Ohio
Client: Conservatory of Music, University of Cincinnati
and Ohio Arts Council
Architect: Pei Cobb Freed & Partners
Engineer: Dewhurst Macfarlane
Design principal: James Carpenter
Senior designer: Stephanie Forsythe
Project team: Katherine Wyberg
Installation: Brian Gulick, Greg Morrell
Glass: Depp Glass
Fittings: Tripyramid Structures

GLASS SCREEN STAIR 1998
Pacific Place, Hong Kong
Architect: Wong & Ouyang
Engineer: David Kufferman
Design principal: James Carpenter
Senior designer: Luke Lowings
Installation: Brian Gulick
Glass: Depp Glass
Fittings: Tripyramid Structures

GLASS TUBE FIELD 1998–2003
Tower Place, London, United Kingdom
Client: Tishman Speyer Realty
Architect: Foster and Partners
Engineer: Ove Arup & Partners
Glass tube manufacturers: Schott Rohrglas,
Vegla Germany, Dupont Advanced Glazing
Products, Pilkington Technical Mirrors
Components: Waagner Biro, Vienna, Austria
Design principal: James Carpenter
Senior designer: Luke Lowings
Project team: Richard Kress, Marek Walczak,
Valerie Spalding

LUMINOUS THRESHOLD 1998–2000
Sydney, Australia
Client: Olympic Coordination Authority, Sydney, Australia
Engineer: Wilde & Woolard Pacific
Atomizing: MEE Industries
Glass: Depp Glass
Heliostat: Bomin Solar
Design principal: James Carpenter
Senior designer: Richard Kress
Project team: Marek Walczak

GLASS VITRINE 1998–2001
New York, New York
Client: Bear Stearns
Architect: Skidmore, Owings & Merrill
Engineer: Buro Happold
Design principal: James Carpenter
Senior designer: Katherine Wyberg
Installation: Brian Gulick

LIGHT AND WATER PAVILIONS PROPOSAL 1998
Riyadh, Saudi Arabia
Client: King Faisal Foundation
Architect: Foster and Partners
Engineer: Buro Happold UK, Buro Happold New York
Fountain: Wet Labs
Design principal: James Carpenter
Senior designer: Richard Kress
Project team: Marek Walczak, Luke Lowings

PHOTOVOLTAIC WALL 1999–2002
Austin Convention Center Atrium, Austin, Texas
Client: City of Austin
Architect: Page Southerland Page
Structural Engineer: Ove Arup & Partners, Matt King
Daylighting: Davidson Norris, Carpenter Norris Consulting
Design principal: James Carpenter,
Senior designer: Marek Walczak
Project team: Richard Kress

LUMINOUS ARC 1996–2001
San Diego Convention Center, San Diego, California
Client: San Diego Redevelopment Agency
Architect: Tucker Sadler Associates
Structural engineer: Martin, Chow & Nakabara
Engineer: Ishler Design and Engineering Associates
Design principal: James Carpenter
Senior designer: Richard Kress
Project team: Rebecca Uss
Installation: Brian Gulick

PRISMATIC GLASS SKYLIGHT 1999–2001
Casey Key, Florida
Client: Private
Architect: Toshiko Mori Architect
Structural engineer: Buro Happold
Design principal: James Carpenter
Senior designer: Katherine Wyberg
Installation: Brian Gulick
Glass: Depp Glass
Fittings: Tripyramid Structures

LIGHT BRIDGE 1997
Berlin, Germany
Client: German Foreign Ministry, Berlin
Architect: Müller Reimann Architekten
Design principal: James Carpenter
Senior designer: Luke Lowings
Project team: Richard Kress

**TULANE UNIVERSITY STUDENT CENTER
PROPOSAL** 1999–2006
New Orleans, Louisiana
Client: Tulane University
Architect: Vincent James Associates Architects, with
James Carpenter Design Associates Inc.
Structural engineer: Ove Arup & Partners
Environmental engineer: Transsolar, Matthias Schuler
Design principal: James Carpenter
Senior designer: Richard Kress
Project team: Dietmar Geiselmann, Nilay Oza, Joe Welker,
Johanna Kindvall, Marek Walczak, Uli Franzel, Stephanie
Hui, Valerie Spalding, Nadine Reuters

MACALESTER COLLEGE 1998
St. Paul, Minnesota
Client: Macalester College
Architect: Shepley Bulfinch
Design principal: James Carpenter
Senior designer: Luke Lowings
Installation: Brian Gulick
Glass: Depp Glass
Fittings: Tripyramid Structures

MIT GARAGE 1999
Cambridge, Massachusetts
Client: Massachusetts Institute of Technology
Architect: Ellenzweig Associates
Design principal: James Carpenter
Senior designer: Marek Walczak

MIT ATRIUM ROOF PROPOSAL 1999
Cambridge, Massachusetts
Client: Massachusetts Institute of Technology, Cambridge
Architect: Ellenzweig Associates
Structural engineer: Schlaich Bergermann und Partner
Mechanical engineer: Ove Arup & Partners
Design principal: James Carpenter
Senior designer: Richard Kress
Project team: Marek Walczak, Nilay Oza, Johanna Kindvall

TIME WARNER BUILDING 1999–2004
Jazz@Lincoln Center double cable-net wall, New York, N Y
Architect: Skidmore, Owings & Merrill
SOM design principal: David Childs
SOM associate designer: Jeff Holms
Structural engineer: Schlaich Bergermann und Partner
Client: The Related Companies, Columbus Center LLC
Glass wall contractor: W&W Glass Systems
Design principal: James Carpenter
Senior designers: Luke Lowings, Charlie Choi
Project team: Richard Kress, Aki Ishida, Joe Welker,
Rayme Kuniyuki

CAST LENS WALL 1999–2001
745 7th Avenue, New York, New York
Architect: Kohn Pedersen Fox
Client: Morgan Stanley Dean Witter
Design principal: James Carpenter
Senior designer: Aki Ishida
Installation: Brian Gulick
Glass: Depp Glass; John Lewis Glass
Fittings: Tripyramid Structures

GLASS COLUMNS 1999–2001
New York, New York
Client: Bear Stearns, New York, New York
Architect: Skidmore, Owings & Merrill
Structural engineer: Buro Happold
Design principal: James Carpenter
Senior designer: Katherine Wyberg
Installation: Brian Gulick

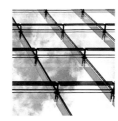

SEATTLE FINANCIAL CENTER 2000–2002
Seattle, Washington
Client: Hines Properties
Architect: Zimmer Gunsul & Frasca Partnership
Design principal: James Carpenter
Senior designer: Richard Kress
Glass: Depp Glass

LUMINOUS BLUE GLASS BRIDGE 2001–2003
Seattle, Washington
Client: City of Seattle, Seattle City Hall
Architect: Bohlin, Cywinsky, Jackson Architects
Structural engineer: Dewhurst Macfarlane
Design principal: James Carpenter
Senior designer: Luke Lowings
Project team: Charlie Choi, Valerie Spalding
Installation: Brian Gulick
Glass: Depp Glass
Fittings: Tripyramid Structures

SCHUBERT CLUB BAND SHELL 2000–2002
Raspberry Island, St. Paul, Minnesota
Client: The Schubert Club, St. Paul
Architect of record: Roark, Kramer, Kosowski Architects,
Peter Kramer
Structural engineer: SOM Engineering William Baker
Consulting engineer: Schlaich Bergermann und Partner
Design principal: James Carpenter
Senior designer: Richard Kress
Project team: Valerie Spalding
Installation: Brian Gulick
Glass: Depp Glass
Fittings: Tripyramid Structures

INCLINED GLASS WALL 1999–2004
New York, New York
Client: New York Hall of Science
Architect: Polshek Partnership
Structural engineer: Andre Chaszar
Design principal: James Carpenter
Senior designer: Richard Kress
Project team: Johanna Kindvall, Marek Walczak, Nilay Oza
Installation: Jim Polk, Chris Vespermann
Fabrication: Canstruct
Glass: Depp Glass

GLASS SCREEN STAIR & SCULPTURAL SKYLIGHT
1999–2001
New York, New York
Client: Private
Structural engineer: Dewhurst Macfarlane
Design principal: James Carpenter
Senior designer: Katherine Wyberg
Installation: Brian Gulick
Glass: Depp Glass
Fittings: Tripyramid Structures

LUMINOUS PORTALS 2000–2005
Ft. Lauderdale Hollywood International Airport, Florida
Architect: Spillis Candela, DMJM
Engineer: David Kufferman
Client: Broward County
Design principal: James Carpenter
Senior designer: Katherine Wyberg
Installation: Brian Gulick
Glass: Depp Glass

PLANTATION PLACE PROPOSAL 1999–2003
London, United Kingdom
Client: British Land PLC
Architect /engineer: Arup Associates
Design principal: James Carpenter
Senior designer: Luke Lowings
Project team: Valerie Spalding

PRIVATE RESIDENCE 2001–2002
Katonah, New York
Client: Private
Architect: Richard Meier & Partners
Engineer: Arup + Partners
Design principal: James Carpenter
Senior designer: Rayme Kuniyuki
Project team: Nilay Oza

MOIRÉ STAIR TOWER 1999–2002
Bonn, Germany
Client: Deutsche Post
Architect: Murphy Jahn Architects, Helmut Jahn
Structural engineer: Sobek Ingenieure, Werner Sobek
Energy/comfort: Transsolar
Design principal: James Carpenter
Senior designer: Richard Kress
Project team: Dietmar Geiselmann

AUDUBON INSECTARIUM 2001
New Orleans, Louisiana
Client: Audubon Society
Design principal: James Carpenter
Senior designer: Rayme Kuniyuki

PEDESTRIAN BRIDGE PROPOSAL 2001
London, United Kingdom
Client: Royal Opera House, London
Design principal: James Carpenter
Senior designer: Luke Lowings
Project team: Valerie Spalding

NORTH CAROLINA MUSEUM PROPOSAL 2001
Raleigh, North Carolina
Client: North Carolina Museum
Architect: Thomas Phifer & Partners
Design principal: James Carpenter
Daylighting: Carpenter Norris Consulting, Davidson Norris

PERISCOPIC VIEWING ROOM 2001 –
Frank E. Moss Federal Courthouse, Salt Lake City, Utah
Client: General Services Administration
Architect: Thomas Phifer and Partners
Design principal: James Carpenter
Senior designer: Richard Kress
Project team: Marek Walczak, Johanna Kindval,
Stephanie Hui

SAN FRANCISCO CONSERVATORY OF MUSIC
PROPOSAL 2001
San Francisco, California
Daylighting: Carpenter Norris Consulting, Davidson Norris
Design principal: James Carpenter
Senior designers: Richard Kress, Davidson Norris

CLOUD PORTAL 2002
New York, New York
Client: Private
Architect: Richard Meier & Partners
Structural engineer: Robert Silman Associates
Design principal: James Carpenter
Senior designer: Rayme Kuniyuki
Installation: Brian Gulick
Fabrication: Lowe Tech Engineering
Glass: Depp Glass

RENEE TABLE 2003
Sarasota, Florida
Client: Private
Honeycomb Glass Composite: Goetz Custom Boats
Design principal: James Carpenter
Senior designer: Katherine Wyberg
Fabrication: Chris Vesperman
Installation: Chris Vespermann

REFLECTIVE CLERESTORY SCULPTURE 2002–2003
Minneapolis, Minnesota
General Mills Atrium
Client: General Mills
Architect: Green & Abrahamson
Glass: Depp Glass
Design principal: James Carpenter
Senior designer: Katherine Wyberg
Installation: Chris Vespermann

7 WORLD TRADE CENTER 2003–2006
New York, New York
Client: Silverstein Properties
Architect: Skidmore, Owings & Merrill
SOM design principal: David Childs
SOM managing principal: T. J. Gottesdiener
SOM technical principal: Carl Galioto
SOM associate partner: Peter Ruggiero
SOM team: Chris Cooper, Ken Lewis, Nick Holt,
Christopher Olson

PODIUM WALL
Design principal: James Carpenter
Senior designer: Richard Kress
Project team: Dietmar Geiselmann, Marek Walczak
Interactive LED consultant: Kinecity Inc., Marek Walczak
Stainless Steel: Johnson Screens
CURTAIN WALL
Design principal: James Carpenter
Senior designer: Richard Kress, Rayme Kuniyuki
Project team: Dietmar Geiselmann, Marek Walczak
Daylight consultant: Carpenter Norris Consulting,
Davidson Norris
Mechanical: Transsolar, Matthias Schuler
LED: LED Effects, Kevin Furry

CABLE NET ENTRY
Design principal: James Carpenter
Project team: Charlie Choi, Joseph Welker, Richard Kress
Structural engineer: Schlaich Bergermann und Partner,
Hans Schober, Stefan Justis
LOBBY WALL
Collaborative artwork with Jenny Holzer
Design principal: James Carpenter
Senior designer: Richard Kress
Project team: Marek Walczak, Johanna Kindvall,
Stephanie Hui
Structural engineer: SOM Engineering, William Baker,
Shane McCormick

SKYGLASS SCREEN WALL 2002
New York, New York
Client: Private
Architect: Richard Meier & Partners
Design principal: James Carpenter
Senior designer: Rayme Kuniyuki
Installation: Brian Gulick
Glass: Depp Glass

SARA LEE BUILDING ENCLOSURE SYSTEMS
2003-2005
Winston Salem, North Carolina
Client: Sara Lee
Architect: Thomas Phifer & Partners
Design principal: James Carpenter
Senior designer: Rayme Kuniyuki
Project team: Richard Kress, Katherine Wyberg, Stephanie
Hui, Jonathan Forsythe, Henrike Bosbach

MUSEUM OF JEWISH HERITAGE 2003-2006
New York, New York
Client: Museum of Jewish Heritage, New York
Design principal: James Carpenter
Senior designers: Richard Kress, Joe Welker
Project team: Stephanie Hui
Interactive consultant: Kinecity, Marek Walczak
LED: LED Effects, Kevin Furry
Glass: Galaxy Glass

AMERICAN UNIVERSITY OF BEIRUT 2002
Beirut, Lebanon
Architect: Vincent James Associates Architects with
James Carpenter Design Associates
Design principal: James Carpenter
Senior designer: Richard Kress
Project team: Dietmar Gieselmann, Aki Ishida,
Katherine Wyberg, Marek Walczak, Uli Franzel
Daylighting: Carpenter Norris Consulting, Davidson Norris

BROOKLYN BRIDGE PARK 2003-2009
New York, New York
Client: Brooklyn Bridge Park Development Corporation
Landscape architect: Michael Van Valkenburgh Associates
Structural engineer: Schlaich Bergermann und Partner,
Hans Schober
Design principal: James Carpenter
Senior designer: Richard Kress
Project team: Johanna Kindvall, Reid Freeman, Emily
Kirkland, Marek Walczak, Rayme Kuniyuki
Energy consultant: Transsolar, Matthias Schuler,
David White

CRAFT MUSEUM PROPOSAL 2002
New York, New York
Client: Museum of Arts and Design
Architect: Toshiko Mori Architect with James Carpenter
Design Associates
Design principal: James Carpenter
Senior designers: Richard Kress, Aki Ishida

LUMINOUS PIER 2003-2005
Chattanooga, Tennessee
Client: City of Chattanooga
Landscape architect: Hargreaves Associates
Design principal: James Carpenter
Senior designers: Joseph Welker, Charlie Choi
Project team: Stephanie Hui, Richard Kress
Fabrication: Johnson Screens

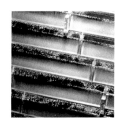

HEARST LIGHT CASCADE 2002-2006
New York, New York
Client: Hearst Corporation
Architect: Foster and Partners
Architect of record: Adamson Associates Architects
Design principal: James Carpenter
Senior designers: Torsten Schlauersbach, Richard Kress
Project team: Johanna Kindvall, Jonathan Forsythe
Water consultant: Fluidity Design Consultants, Jim Garland
Glass: John Lewis Glass

GUCCI GINZA 2004-2006
Tokyo, Japan
Client: Gucci Group Japan
Architect: Obayashi Corporation
Design principal: James Carpenter
Senior designer: Rayme Kuniyuki
Project team: Dorothy Schmidinger, Jonathan Forsythe,
Richard Kress, Charlie Choi, Stephanie Hui

HOBOKEN CITY PIER C PARK 2002-2006
Hoboken, New Jersey
Client: City of Hoboken
Landscape architect: Michael Van Valkenburgh &
Associates
Structural engineer: SOM Engineering, William Baker,
Shane McCormack
Design principal: James Carpenter
Senior designers: Richard Kress, Charlie Choi
Project team: Johanna Kindvall, Torsten Schlauersbach,
Rayme Kuniyuki

SMITHSONIAN NATIONAL PORTRAIT MUSEUM
EXPANSION PROPOSAL 2003
Washington, District of Columbia
Client: Smithsonian Institution, Washington DC
Architect: Toshiko Mori Architect with JCDA
Design principal: James Carpenter
Senior designers: Rayme Kuniyuki
Project team: Joseph Welker, Katherine Wyberg,
Cameron Wu, Richard Kress

GALLERY SKYLIGHT PROPOSAL 2003
Napa, California
Client: Private
Architect: Rick Joy Architects
Design principal: James Carpenter
Senior designer: Richard Kress
Project team: Joseph Welker, Uli Franzel

SOLAR REFLECTOR SHELL 2004-
New York, New York
Client: MTA Arts in Transit and the City of New York
Department of Design and Construction
Architect: Nicholas Grimshaw & Partners
Structural engineer: Ove Arup & Partners
Daylight consultant: Carpenter Norris Consulting,
Davidson Norris
Design principal: James Carpenter
Senior designer: Richard Kress
Project team: Joseph Welker, Marek Walczak, Stephanie
Hui, Johanna Kindvall, Eva Rothmeier, Torsten
Schlauersbach, Rayme Kuniyuki

BATTERY PARK CITY STREETSCAPE
2004–2006
New York, New York
Client: Battery Park City Authority
Architect: Rogers Marvel Architects
Structural engineer: Robert Silman Associates
Design principal: James Carpenter
Senior designer: Joseph Welker
Project team: Johanna Kindvall
Glass: John Lewis Glass
Metal Fabrication: Johnson Screens

MACKLOWE RESIDENCE 2005
New York, New York
Client: Macklowe Properties
Design principal: James Carpenter
Senior designer: Rayme Kuniyuki
Project team: Stephanie Hui

LUMINOUS CUBE 2005–2006
Haghetaot, Israel
Client: The Ghetto Fighters' Museum at Beit Lohamei
Architect: Efrat Kowalsky, Architects
Design principal: James Carpenter
Senior designer: Torsten Schlauersbach
Project team: Jonathan Forsythe

DANIEL PATRICK MOYNIHAN STATION 2005–
New York, New York
Client: Vornado Realty Trust and The Related Companies
Executive architect: HOK
Project Designers: James Carpenter Design Associates
Design principal: James Carpenter
Senior designers: Joseph Welker, Richard Kress,
Reid Freedman
Project team: Torsten Schlauersbach, Johanna Kindvall,
Kate Wyberg, Cameron Wu, Devin Hines
Structural engineer: Hans Schober, Schlaich Bergermann
und Partner

ISRAEL MUSEUM 2005–2010
Jerusalem, Israel
Client: Israel Museum
Executive architect: Lerman Architects
Planning architect: Efrat Kowalsky, Architects
Design principal: James Carpenter
Senior designers: Reid Freeman
Project team: Richard Kress, Cameron Wu, Johanna
Kindvall, Stephanie Hui, Eva Rothmeier

MADISON SQUARE GARDEN RENOVATION 2005
New York, New York
Client: Madison Square Garden
Architect: Gensler
Design principal: James Carpenter
Project team: Richard Kress, Cameron Wu, Joseph Welker

^ Photograph of Dr. Robert J. Carpenter (7th from left) with Dr. Alexander Graham Bell (5th from left), July 14, 1908, Beinn Bhreagh, Cape Breton, Nova Scotia

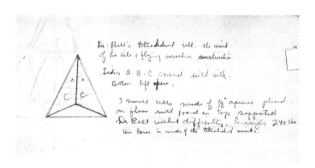

^ Sketch by Dr. Robert J. Carpenter of a tetrahedral cell structure of Dr. Bell's kites and fly-ing machines. 3 sides, A, B & C covered in silk, D left open, structure of 1/8 inch (3mm) planed spruce.

There are four groups of people I want to thank.

My first acknowledgment is to James Carpenter, for the spirit of collaboration maintained throughout the book's progress. Our conversations about his work have brought my attention to subtle phenomena within the environment. The conceptual strength of his projects has provoked my thesis as a way to capture his contribution to an emergent redefinition of design practices. The book would not have been possible without the steady and exacting participation of Ben Colebrook, who has assisted Jamie and me since its onset. He has supervised the organization of all visual and written materials from within JCDA, researching, gathering, laying out, and giving consistency to a vast body of work.

The second group of people includes the two eminent contributors Jorg Schlaich and Ken Frampton. The professional association among Jorg and Jamie qualifies the distinction and convergence between an engineering pursuit of absolute reductionism, and the identification of minimal deviations from this pursuit of necessity, that introduce a further degree of aesthetic experience. Ken's commitment to an environmental agenda in architecture has resulted in a detailed and comprehensive reading of JCDA's most recent work, by tracing its trajectory from an affinity with engineering to the deployment of environmental thinking. Other friends and colleagues have offered insightful comments and advice, including Sebastien Marot, Mary Miss, Alessandra Ponte, Julio Salcedo, Els Verbakel, Mirko Zardini, Sarah Whiting, and Gwendolyn Wright.

The third group of people I want to thank are the authors of the diagrams that substantiate the book's thesis. Uli Franzel worked during the initial stages of the book's development, contributing to its conception and fine-tuning the optical diagrams of the projects chosen as paradigms for the first chapter. Cameron Wu brought into the picture his exquisite sensibility, to bridge the difficult pairing of filmic and architectural works selected as paradigms for the book's third chapter. His diagrams establish a conceptual relationship between heterogeneous materials, reflecting his special way of looking at the world, which is both attuned to contemporary conditions of mediated reality and committed to a pursuit of architecture.

Laura Crescimano requires a special acknowledgment alongside this group, not only because of her extensive contribution in diagramming the paradigm chosen for the second chapter, but also on more fronts of collaboration. She took on the work of helping to clarify my intellectual agenda by reprocessing and bringing to a new level all of the projects' materials that I had selected. Her support and availability for discussion enabled me to refine the book's narrative line: in this sense she could be credited as conceptual designer and co-editor. Without her participation and skills in fostering communication among the various members of the team, you might not be reading these pages.

The fourth group of people includes the editor at Birkhäuser and the graphic designer, who have assisted, supported, questioned, and propelled from Germany the work that was being done in New York. Ria Stein has demonstrated an almost supernatural level of patience and belief in this book as it inched its way towards completion. Silke Nalbach responded graphically to Jamie's and my pursuit of simplicity—not an easy goal to accomplish considering the material's heterogeneity—working with great precision during the final phase of the work.

There is no category of acknowledgment that could describe my indebtedness to Linda Pollak, who encouraged me to take on the challenge of writing the first monograph on Jamie's work, read and commented upon my early notes, and has remained very close to both the work ever since. Many of the ideas I put forth here are the outcome of our intellectual, professional, and personal association. As in most of her undertakings, Linda has exceeded any expectations as a uniquely insightful editor of both ideas and language, as patient colleague in the office, and in the incommensurable role of muse.

Sandro Marpillero
February 2006

Our design studio has always been an environment that encourages collaboration between studio designers, engineers, architects, landscape architects and fabricators. As such, over the past 27 years, there have been numerous participants in a wide range of projects. Within the studio, the long term contributions of Richard Kress and Luke Lowings have been most significant. Current studio members include Reid Freeman, Brian Gulick, Stephanie Hui, Emily Kirkland, Richard Kress, Rayme Kuniyuki, Eva Rothmeier, Torsten Schlauersbach, Marek Walczak, Joseph Welker, Cameron Wu and Katharine Wyberg. No office can function or grow without the hard work of its office staff. Office Manager since 1997, Diane Chillog is of particular importance to JCDA's success, meanwhile as Administrator, MiYoung Sohn supports the office in multiple capacities.

Long term collaborations with structural engineers including Tony Broomhead, Jörg Schlaich, Hans Schober, Bill Baker, Tim Macfarlane and Werner Sobek have provided inspiration and clarity to many of our projects. The close involvement of our fabricators including Tim Eliassen, Michael Mulhearn and Wesley Depp have allowed us to fully realize the work at a level of execution that would not otherwise have been possible. James Carpenter Design has grown over the years to produce Carpenter Norris Consulting, a daylighting consulting firm consisting of James Carpenter and Davidson Norris, and Carpenter Lowings, a London-based architecture firm specializing in glass and architecture consisting of Luke Lowings and James Carpenter. JCDA's relationship with Matthias Schuler of Transsolar is another key collaboration which has assisted JCDA's ambition to integrate ecological, artistic and architectural design.

To all of our clients and architect collaborators, the opportunities given have been challenging and productive and we hope to continue the level of engagement in projects that can produce exceptional works in the public realm.

James Carpenter
January 2006

Past Studio Members:
Rachel Berwick
Henrike Bosbach
Martha Bush
Charlie Choi
Binda Colebrook
Peter Drobny
Erica Friedman
Jonathan Forsythe
Stephanie Forsythe
Janet Fink
Uli Franzel
Anne Gardiner
Liesl Geiger
Dietmar Geiselman
Katherine Gormley
Devin Hines
Aki Ishida
Johanna Kindvall
Neil Logan
Nilay Oza
Daniel Reiser
Dan Trupiano
Vera Marjonovic
Mark McClellan
Greg Morrell
Michael Morris
Yoshiko Sato
Dorothy Schmidinger
Valerie Spalding
Mary Springer
Stephanie Snyder
Rebecca Uss
Georgia Van Ryzin
Kate Wall
Maria Westerphal